Bates Torrey

A Road Book for Cycling and Carriage Driving in Maine

Bates Torrey

A Road Book for Cycling and Carriage Driving in Maine

ISBN/EAN: 9783337419936

Printed in Europe, USA, Canada, Australia, Japan

Cover: Foto ©Andreas Hilbeck / pixelio.de

More available books at **www.hansebooks.com**

A

FOR

CYCLING AND CARRIAGE DRIVING IN MAINE

BATES TORREY

(Second Edition, Revised)

PORTLAND, MAINE
STEVENS & JONES CO., PUBLISHERS
1895

BICYCLES AND SUNDRIES

WHOLESALE AGENTS FOR

STANDARD CYCLOMETERS, WEBB'S CYCLE PREPARATIONS AND ALL BICYCLE NECESSITIES.

MONARCH
BICYCLES

RENTING

and TEACHING

IN THE HALL.

Send difficult repairing and orders for any sundries to

HAGGETT BROTHERS,

Union Hall,   143 Free Street,   PORTLAND.

INTRODUCTORY.

THE Routes set forth in this book have been compiled from information obtained from many sources, but mostly from wheelmen. The endeavor has been to describe actual wheeling experiences.

The condition of a road will vary from year to year, and a description of its surface should therefore be taken with some allowance. A glance at the topography of Maine will be sufficient to convince any one that perfect roads and perfect scenery must be incompatible — in this country where road building has not become an exact science. The rugged coast of Maine, so strangely indented; its water courses, commercial and sylvan; the magnificent lakes — all are wonderful, and for the tourist their grandeur and beauty go far to mitigate roughness of the roads. Every hill has its valley, and from the height the prospect is sure to be inviting; almost every sandy stretch has its by-path which the astute bicyclist is quick to discover; every rolling road along shore is in touch with rural scenes, and the proximity of the sea gives invigoration.

The first edition of this road-book appeared before the advent of the pneumatic tire, which has done so much to change the point of view, and render so many erstwhile rough places comparatively smooth. Under present conditions Maine is a far more rideable state than formerly, and if a comparison be made, its interior and northern portions average better than along the coast. But all in all its compensations are enough to make apology or criticism unnecessary. Hundreds of thousands visit Maine annually for health, recreation, or sport, and not one departs unsatisfied.

BATES TORREY.

MAINE LOCAL CONSULS, 1895.

Auburn	H. L. Burr.	Fairfield	John P. Lawry.	Perry	Justin E. Gove.
Augusta	Julian Wilder.	Farmington	Geo. McL. Presson.	Portland	C. M. P. Steele.
Bath	S. Cuyler Greene.	Gardiner	John W. Berry.	Presque Isle	Leon S. Howe.
Bangor	Charles H. Barstow.	Guilford	S. C. Bennett.	Richmond	T. J. Southard, 2d.
Belfast	William M. Thayer.	Hallowell	John Robinson.	Rockland	C. M. Robinson.
Bethel	S. N. Buck.	Houlton	W. S. Lewin.	Saco	N. D. Colcord.
Biddeford	N. D. Colcord.	Kennebunk	Geo. W. Larrabee.	Sanford	C. A. Bodwell.
Bridgton	H. C. Gibbs.	Kittery	Fred E. Dixon.	Skowhegan	Roland T. Patten.
Brunswick	George F. Tenney.	Lewiston	J. W. Hartley.	South Norridgewock	Dr. W. F. Brown.
Buckfield	Fred H. Atwood.	Lisbon Falls	Alfred R. Brendel.	South Paris	F. E. Kimball.
Calais	Horace G. Trimble.	Morrill	H. Merriman.	Springvale	F C. Bradeen.
Castine	Guy A. Sargent.	New Vineyard	Bruce C. Jacobs.	Vinalhaven	Frank H. Wharff.
Cornish	W. T. S. Morrison.	Norway	L. P. Swett.	Waldoboro	E. A. Glidden.
East Pittston	H. A. Clark.	Oakland	J. Henry Morse.	Waterville	H. C. Prince.
Eastport	S. P. Bradish.	Oldtown	L. A. Farrell.	Yarmouthville	Frank A. Pendexter.
Ellsworth	John A. Hale.	Paris	George M. Atwood.		

BY-LAWS
OF THE
MAINE DIVISION, L. A. W.
ORGANIZED AT PORTLAND, MAY 20, 1886.

By-Laws Revised May 30, 1890.

ARTICLE I. — The object of this Division is to promote the general interests of wheeling in Maine.

ARTICLE II. — *Section 1.* In accordance with Article IV. of the Constitution of the League of American Wheelmen, the Officers of the Division shall consist of a Chief Consul, Vice Consul, Representative or Representatives, and a Secretary-Treasurer.

Section 2. These Officers shall constitute the Executive Board, and shall have charge of all affairs of the Division.

ARTICLE III. — *Section 1.* The Chief Consul shall preside at all meetings of the Division, and of the Executive Board; shall fill *pro tempore* any vacancy in any office or committee until the next ensuing regular meeting of the Division, when suc vacancy shall be filled in the same manner as provided for at annual elections; and shall call special meetings of the Division when he shall deem it necessary. At the request of any twelve members, the Chief Consul shall call a special meeting, of which at least six days' notice shall be given to each member.

Section 2. In the absence or illness of the Chief Consul, the Vice Consul shall fulfill the duties of the office of Chief Consul.

Section 3. The Secretary-Treasurer shall notify each member of all meetings, and pay all bills which have been approved by the Executive Board.

ARTICLE IV. — *Section 1.* The annual meeting (Fall Meet) shall be held on Labor Day in each year, at such place as the Executive Board may decide, and each member shall be notified of this meeting at least two weeks previous thereto. At this meeting the order of business shall be as follows: —

    Reading of records of previous annual meeting.
    Reports of Chief Consul, Representatives, and Secretary-Treasurer.
    Motions, votes and resolutions.

Section 2. A special meeting (Spring Meet) shall be held on Memorial Day of each year.

ARTICLE V. — At all meetings of this Division fifteen members shall constitute a quorum, but a less number may meet and adjourn.

ARTICLE VI. — Alterations or amendments to these rules may be made at any meeting of the Division, provided notice of such amendment shall be sent to each member at least ten days previous to such meeting.

EXPLANATION.

THE limited space at command is the excuse for some omissions. The "Specific Directions" are intended for the most part to assist in riding out of cities and towns, and to indicate the route where particular direction may be needed. To be more explicit would cumber the book with details as likely to mystify as to enlighten.

Naming the towns passed through will serve to call attention to the main roads between them, and the much travelled highways are easily distinguishable from those less important.

A fuller description of roads, grades and surfaces would signify nothing, because changes are bound to occur from year to year.

As regards distances — that is a tender spot in the vitals of a Road Book. We hope these are correct; we have confidence that from the mass of material examined, they have been made approximate; we sincerely trust that none are wide from the truth.

Turns right or left are indicated by the letters R. or L. A fork of the road by the letter Y.

Hotel rates are L. A. W. as far as possible to obtain. A careful examination of the Index and Maps is recommended to those who would plan routes or combinations of routes.

PORTSMOUTH, N. H., TO BIDDEFORD.

THROUGH ROUTE   **No. 1.**

Specific Directions.	Pass Through.	Road.	Distance.
Follow Shore Road N.E. The Beaches at York, Ogunquit, Wells and Kennebunkport can be reached about a mile to R. of this route. See pages 8, 9, 15, and 16.	York. Ogunquit. Wells Village. Kennebunk. *Biddeford.*	Very sandy and rough.	8 Miles. 8½ " 5½ " 5 " 9 "
			36 Miles.

This is not a most favorable introduction to Maine roads, but they improve upon more acquaintance. Perhaps a better entry to the State by wheel is by way of Dover or Rochester, described under Routes Nos. 2 and 3.

BIDDEFORD TO BIDDEFORD POOL (9 m.) — Leaving Hotel Thacher, proceed toward South Biddeford by way of Main, Alfred, and Pool streets. Over a good road, through plenty of fine country, with ocean views all along the way. Good fishing, boating, and bathing at the Pool. Fine mile stretch across the marsh. Another direction, — follow the telegraph poles.

BIDDEFORD TO OLD ORCHARD (5 m.) — Leave Hotel Thacher east by way of Lincoln street; cross bridge to Elm (Saco 1 m.), then Beach street and Old Orchard Road to Old Orchard. Road a trifle sandy in places, but can be easily ridden. Old Orchard has an unrivaled beach, — a seven mile extent of hard, smooth sand. A most popular resort, with at least twenty-five hotels, and best facilities for surf bathing, etc.

HOTELS — PORTSMOUTH, Kearsarge House, $2.50. BIDDEFORD, Hotel Thacher, $2.00. Keep off sidewalks. Bicycle club at Biddeford the York County Wheelmen, who are wonderfully enterprising, and are always pleased to receive visitors at their club rooms on Main street.

DOVER, N. H., TO BIDDEFORD.

THROUGH ROUTE — No. 2.

SPECIFIC DIRECTIONS.	PASS THROUGH.	ROAD.	DISTANCE.
Leave Dover by turnpike road to South Berwick, entering that town at South Berwick Landing. Then turn L. to Main street; proceed by way of——	South Berwick. North " Wells Village. Kennebunk. ***Biddeford.***	Fair. Hilly. Sandy.	5 Miles. 7 " 9 " 5 " 9 "
			35 Miles.

[SPECIFIC DIRECTIONS CONTINUED.]—Portland street direct to North Berwick, striking Elm; then R. to Wells street, and R. to Market to Post Office. Cross railroad to go to Varney House. One mile may be saved by turning R. from Elm street just before entering North Berwick, and joining Wells street as it issues from the town extending toward Wells. Leave North Berwick by Portland street to Wells, then straight to "Merriland Ridge," so called, and L. to Wells. From thence straight road through Kennebunk to Biddeford. Within 2 miles of North Berwick is Great Hill, which is not rideable. Another smaller hill occurs farther along the road.

KENNEBUNK TO KENNEBUNKPORT, (4 m. S. E.)—Latter place is a fashionable resort and growing in importance. Hotel, Parker House, $2.00. Good boating and bathing. Turn R. to bluff—fair road.

NORTH BERWICK—Varney House, $1.00. BERWICK—Grant's, $2.00. WELLS—Hotel Matthews, $1.00. KENNEBUNK—Mousam House, $1.50.

ROCHESTER, N. H., TO BIDDEFORD.

Through Route   **No. 3.**

Specific Directions.	Pass Through.	Road.	Distance.
Start—Dodge's hotel, take Summer street, cross railroad track, proceed about 100 yards, turn L. then R., and direct to E. Rochester; Main street, turn L., cross bridge go direct to S. Lebanon schoolhouse, 1 mile.——	E. Rochester. S. Lebanon. Lebanon. *Sanford.* Alfred. Lyman. *Biddeford.*	Hilly.	3 Miles. 14 " 5 " 13 " 35 Miles.

[SPECIFIC DIRECTIONS CONTINUED.] — Turn L. then first and second R. on through "Guinea Woods" to white house on corner about 5 m. from E. Rochester; then turn R. then L. direct to store near East Lebanon Depot; then L. across track, and to Sanford over Mount Hope.

SANFORD TO BIDDEFORD. — Same as Route No. 6.

SANFORD TO KENNEBUNK. — Follow Alfred Road 2½ m., then L. for short distance, then sharp R. and direct to Whicher's Mills; then ¼ m. beyond (near lumber yards) turn R. and proceed direct to Kennebunk Depot (13 m.); from thence direct to Kennebunk. 4 m. farther to Kennebunkport, a beautiful summer resort; Parker House, $2.00.
9 m. from Sanford, on the road to Kennebunk keep sharp lookout at R. for road into woods which leads to Steep Falls on Mousam River. See guide-board marked "Old Falls." The place is worth a visit.

SANFORD TO ALFRED. — Washington street, then turn R. after crossing bridge; two bad hills will be encountered farther on. Turn sharp L. in woods, and direct to Alfred.

SANFORD TO WELLS BEACH, via Wells Depot (9½ m.), and WELLS VILLAGE (4½ m.). Leave via School street, across Butler Bridge, taking Main road at foot of Lyon Hill (4 m.). Good bathing and fishing at beach.

ROCHESTER, N.H., TO CORNISH.

THROUGH ROUTE.   No. 4.

SPECIFIC DIRECTIONS.	PASS THROUGH.	ROAD.	DISTANCE.
Rochester to Sanford by Route No. 3.	*Sanford.*	Hilly	14 Miles.
	Springvale.		2 "
	Emery Mills.	good	3½ "
	Shapleigh.	up grade.	3½ "
A more direct route may be noted below.	Newfield.	Sandy.	8 "
	Limerick.	Easy	4 "
	Cornish.	run.	10 "
			45 Miles.

THE MORE DIRECT WAY from SPRINGVALE to CORNISH is through the township of WATERBOROUGH. Leave Springvale Depot by Guinea Road to Alfred Gore (road) (4 m.); thence to Ross Corner (5 m.), Things Mills (2 m.), over Clark's Bridge on to Limerick (5 m.), and Cornish (10 m.). Total distance 26 m. The former route is more picturesque, but this latter is shorter and with more level roads.

NOTE.— While the above is the nearer route, yet it traverses some cross roads, and for that reason may be hard to follow. The road most settled is the old stage route from Sanford to Cornish, via Alfred (5 m.), South Waterborough (4 m), Waterborough Center (4 m.), Limerick (7 m.) to Cornish (10 m.). Total 30 m.

CORNISH TO SACO (30 m.) — Pass through Limington Corner (8 m.), from thence direct road to Edgecomb's Bridge and through North Hollis to Hollis Center (11 m.); thence to Salmon Falls (2 m.), and Saco (9 m.). Road a trifle hilly at beginning, but excellent afterward. Enter Saco by North St.

SACO TO WHITE MOUNTAINS. — Reverse route last above, and from CORNISH to CRAWFORD NOTCH take Route No. 5.

CORNISH SIDE-RUNS.

CORNISH TO LIMERICK (10 m.) — Leave town by Main street, cross bridge at Eagle Mills to Maple street, take second left-hand road. Keep main travelled road.

CORNISH TO FREEDOM (12 m.) — Up the Ossipee Valley by way of Kezar Falls (4 m.), Porter (2 m.), Hunt's Bridge (2 m.), Freedom (4 m.).

CORNISH TO SPECTACLE PONDS (5 m.) — Leave town by Main and Maple streets. Keep straight on past Fair Grounds to Kezar Falls. Turn right front of Post Office, go through covered bridge and keep straight road, by way of Kezar Falls or South Hiram.

CORNISH TO BROWNFIELD (14 m.) — Leave town by Main and Maple streets. Turn right at Pike Cottage. Leave Fair Grounds and Cemetery to the left; go down steep hill and through Warren's Bridge. Keep main road and follow river until you strike Brownfield Road, then go through Notch, etc. The best on account of its varied scenery.

CORNISH TO HIRAM FALLS (4 m.) — Leave town by Bridge street, go through bridge across Ossipee River, thence by main road to Hiram, etc. The largest fall on the Saco; the river here leaps off ragged ledges, and falls 85 ft. Mt. Cutler 2 m. up, on the banks of the Saco. Hotel at base of mountain.

CORNISH TO DENMARK (12 m.) — Leave town same as Hiram Falls, then by way of Hiram Bridge, East Hiram, and Bull-ring road.

CORNISH TO BRIDGTON (21 m.) — Via Hiram and Denmark.

CORNISH SIDE-RUNS. — (*Continued.*)

CORNISH TO SANDY BEACH (15 m.) — Leave town by Cumberland "Stage Road" to Cornish Station, thence by river road to double R.R. crossing near East Baldwin; through Smut street to Sebago road, turn sharp left and keep main road to East Sebago, etc. Finest view of Sebago Lake. Elegant roads.

CORNISH TO CLARK MT. — Cornish to Long Pond, Cornish to Devil's Den, caves, and cart-roads in the solid rock (a wonderful sight) are other side-runs which may be taken.

BATH TO BIRCH POINT (8 m.). — Start at Court H., High street through Winnegance to Campbell's Pond, then first L. to Point. Elbow Hill just beyond Pond a trifle dangerous. Be careful when turning on the slope.

BATH TO SMALL POINT, FORT POPHAM, AND POPHAM BEACH. — High street to Winnegance, then R. after crossing bridge, straight to Phipsburg Centre, beyond which take L. of Y. and bear to L. for Small Pt. (about 16 m.); or R. of Y. and bear to R. for Popham Beach (16 m.).

Every bicyclist should join the L. A. W. By such action he becomes a member of an influential body of wheelmen, and the spirit of fraternity that is fostered is no less pleasing than to have a share in the movements which the League has been and is identified with. One wheelman can work for his own good, and the good of his community; but many thousand wheelmen can become a power in the land, and benefit the masses.

Every member of the L. A. W., should take the cue from those active in the organization and agitate for better roads. "Better roads" is and should be the war cry. The L. A. W. has become a large organization, and it can be made a powerful one. Legislatures have been influenced by it; but aside from large reforms each and every member can do his little, and rest satisfied that he is benefiting the community quite as much as himself.

CORNISH TO WHITE MOUNTAINS.

THROUGH ROUTE.   NO. 5.

SPECIFIC DIRECTIONS.	PASS THROUGH.	ROAD.	DISTANCE.
This is the direct route.	South Hiram.	Medium.	3½ miles.
	Brownfield.	Excellent.	10 "
	Conway Centre.	Hilly.	10 "
	Red Stone.	Sandy.	4 "
	North Conway.	Good.	2 "
	Intervale.	"	3 "
	Glen Station.	"	3 "
	Bartlett.	Medium.	11 "
	Crawford Notch and House.	All up grade.	12 "
			58½ miles.

This route extends somewhat into New Hampshire, but is presented for the benefit of touring wheelmen from the South and West who have the White Mountains as their objective point; whether they come by way of Portland, Saco, or Rochester.

ANOTHER WAY.—From Cornish the White Mountains may be reached via Fryeburg, which is a historic old town that ought to be visited. The tourist ought to take the trip around the river, visit Martha's Grove, where the Camp Meeting is annually in session, and see the largest detached bowlder in America. All this can be accomplished by leaving direct route at Brownfield, passing through the "Notch," and taking the Old Country road to Fryeburg (6 m.). To resume the journey cross Weston's Bridge and follow the Saco, striking the Through Route just south of Red Stone, thus avoiding the sandy road between Fryeburg and Conway Center.

MILTON MILLS, N. H., TO BIDDEFORD.

THROUGH ROUTE   **No. 6.**

SPECIFIC DIRECTIONS.	PASS THROUGH.	ROAD.	DISTANCE.
Take main road to Fair Ground near Long Pond, then turn R. to bridge (3m) and L. as you coast the short hill in front of store. Then keep main road to Springvale and Sanford Here take Washington street across bridge and turn R. to "Hardscrabble," and so on direct to Alfred.	South Acton. Emery's Mills. Springvale. Sanford. Alfred. Lyman. *Biddeford.*	Hilly.	3 miles. 3½ " 3½ " 2 " 5 " 4 " 9 "
			30 Miles.

[SPECIFIC DIRECTIONS CONTINUED.] Or turn sharp to L. in front of Hotel Brown at Springvale, and ride to R. R. Station; thence bearing L. by Fair Ground to Shaw's Ridge, which saves a mile, but is a harder road to Alfred.

Straight road from ALFRED TO BIDDEFORD. Avoid all turns. Good coast as approach city. Look out for Raccoon Gully a few miles beyond ALFRED. [Grade of Gully since improved.]

Good black bass fishing in Long Pond, and excellent opportunity for rowing, boating and bathing. Picturesque scenery, but no hotel.

SHAPLEIGH CORNER north of EMERY'S MILLS, (3½ m.). ACTON CORNER N. W. of EMERY'S MILLS, (3½ m.) At ALFRED, county buildings and jail. SHAKER VILLAGE about 1½ m. N. Hotel, Central House, L. A. W. $1.00. SPRINGVALE, L. A. W. Hotel, Springvale House, $1.00. SANFORD, L. A. W. Hotel, Hotel Sanford, $1.50.

YORK COUNTY SIDE-RUNS.

SANFORD TO NORTH BERWICK.—Start North Berwick street, keep main road until after crossing bridge at Morrill's Mills, then bear to R. and follow direct road which is good for 6 m., then sandy. Distance 10 m.

SANFORD TO BERWICK AND GREAT FALLS, (15½ m.)—Start same as above; when near Bauneg Beg Pond (4 m.) notice guide post, turn R. then bear L. and keep main road. After crossing bridge notice signboard "South Berwick 7 m." here bear R. By taking South Berwick road at this point will get better going, though distance several miles farther. Berwick and Great Falls connected by bridge. L. A. W. Hotel, Great Falls House, $2.00.

NORTH BERWICK TO YORK BEACH.—Leave Varney House, crossing railroad track to Market Square. Turn L. to Elm street, [2 m.] to Great Hill, then L. to Emery's Bridge Meeting House, after which L. for a few rods, then R. to Hooper's Saw Mill, which is nearest point to Mt. Agamenticus, the highest point in this region, and one mile distant from road. No wheel road to the mountain. Proceed through York Woods to four corners, then L. direct to York Beach, 18 miles.

Another route to York Beach is to follow Ogunquit road about 6 m., then turn R., Mt. Agamenticus being about 4 m. distant toward the west. Fair road, and about same distance.

NORTH BERWICK TO OGUNQUIT.—Market street, directly S. E. through what is called in local parlance "Tacknic" (Post Office, Berwick Branch). A pleasant run, distance 9 m. Bald Head Cliff about ¼ m. from Ogunquit.

NORTH BERWICK TO WELLS BEACH.—R. to Wells street, then L. to "Merriland Ridge," R., over R. R., and L. to Wells Village and Beach. Distance 11 m. At Wells there are two beaches, upper and lower, each about 2 m. long. Good trout fishing in Branch Brook [6 m.].

OGUNQUIT, Maxwell House, $. WELLS, Bay View, $.

BIDDEFORD TO PORTLAND.

THROUGH ROUTE   **No. 7.**

SPECIFIC DIRECTIONS.	PASS THROUGH.	ROAD.	DISTANCE.
Biddeford House to Bridge, which cross into Saco, then L. to Elm street, leaving Saco by way of Main street, and following shore road to Portland. Enter Portland by way of Vaughan——	*Saco.* Dunstan's Corner. Oak Hill. Cash's Corner. *Portland.*	Good average road.	1 Mile. 6 " 3 " 6 " 16 Miles.

[SPECIFIC DIRECTIONS CONTINUED.]—Bridge, Danforth street, L. to Emery, R. to Pine, so on to Congress street, and Preble House.

OLD ORCHARD may be reached from this route by turning R. toward south at Schoolhouse No. 4, about 4 miles from Saco. Distance to Beach about 2½ miles. Sidewalks can be ridden on Beach street, Saco, from brick schoolhouse to cemetery, providing due care be exercised. Road bad there. Fiske Hotel, L. A. W.

FOR PINE POINT.—Turn R. at Dunstan's Corner. Beach about 2½ miles from the main road.

FOR PROUT'S NECK, or Checkley House (L. A. W.)—Turn R. at Oak Hill; distance about 4 m. These roads to the beaches are fair, with down grades.

SACO, L. A. W. hotel, Saco House. $1.50

The highway from Biddeford to Portland is generally good; the grades are all easy, and it is considered a good run. Portland, Preble House, L. A. W., $2.50,

For side runs from Portland, see following pages, 19 to 22, 24 to 30, inclusive.

BIDDEFORD SIDE-RUNS.

BIDDEFORD TO SACO FERRY (5 m.) — Follow electric road which runs to Old Orchard, but branch off at Cemetery where signboard reads "Beach Road." At ferry will be found summer-house of the York County Wheelmen. This is a popular run, over good roads.

BIDDEFORD TO SEBAGO LAKE (22 m.) — Enter Saco according to specific directions of Route No. 7. Leave Saco by North street. Proceed on Saco side of the river, going north-west, and passing through Buxton Lower Corner (9 m.), Buxton Center (3 m.), York's Corner (2 m.), Standish Corner (6 m.) to Sebago Lake (2 m.). At Buxton Lower Corner is Sanderson's Public House.

BIDDEFORD TO ALFRED (14 m.) — Leave city through Elm street to Five Points; turn to right (Alfred Road), thence straight. Rather hilly, but pretty fair surface.

BIDDEFORD TO GOODWIN'S MILLS (6 m.) — Leave city by South or Main street; continue straight road 2½ m. to fork of roads with tree in fork; turn L. at this Y, and proceed straight.

BIDDEFORD TO HILL'S BEACH. — Main street to Alfred to Pool street. Turn L. near signboard "Fort Hill," 5½ m. from Biddeford. Summer-house of York County Wheelmen, across the river, can be reached by ferry.

BIDDEFORD SIDE-RUNS. (*Continued.*)

BIDDEFORD TO KENNEBUNKPORT (10 m.) — Leave Biddeford by Elm street to West Biddeford; turn L. just beyond overhead R.R. bridge; keep to the left, nearly a straight road. Rather sandy, but side-paths a part of the way.

BIDDEFORD TO GOOSE ROCKS (10 m.) — Leave city by Main, Alfred, Birch, Granite and West streets; follow West street southeast 3 m. to schoolhouse; then turn R., take first road L.; ride to Ridge Meeting-house, and take first easterly road; then straight to brick basement house; turn R.; take first road to left. At this resort hotel accommodations are good, with plenty of boating, gunning, and fishing.

BIDDEFORD TO FORTUNE'S ROCKS (10 m.) — Route same as to Pool, except turn sharp R. at beach bridge (within view of ocean); across beach 2 m. The same point may be reached by following Goose Rocks route as far as schoolhouse; keep straight road by schoolhouse through the woods; then turn sharp R., and hold to left by Curtis Farm.

BIDDEFORD TO PINE POINT. — Same route as to Old Orchard, following beach road from Old Orchard, 3 m. Another route is: Saco to Dunstan via Portland Road, holding to L. at point where roads diverge, about 1 m. from Saco city building; at Dunstan (7 m.) turn R. straight road to sea. Shore dinners and board may be obtained here.

PORTLAND TO OCEAN HOUSE, CAPE ELIZABETH.

Side Run (VIA SHORE ROAD.) No 6.

Specific Directions.	Pass By.	Road.	Distance.
Leave Portland by Cape Elizabeth Ferry to South Portland, turn first L. after landing, proceed via Spring street to "Willard," then L. by Shore Road making all important turns L.—	Cape Cottage. Portland Headlight. Delano Park. Pond Cove. *Ocean House.*	Generally good, some hills, all rideable.	3½ Miles. 1 " 3 " 8 Miles.

[Specific Directions Continued.]—Or proceed straight from the ferry, and ascend quite a hill just outside of the village, then bear always to L.

Or leave Portland by way of Congress, State and York streets to Portland Bridge, continuing through the village of Knightville, turning L. at the schoolhouse, and on over Meeting House Hill upon the "Shore" (Cottage) Road, or R., which is the Ocean House Road by Cape Elizabeth town-house, and which connects with Shore Road by turning L. at Pond Cove Schoolhouse, so called, about 5 m. from Knightville.

Cape Cottage location, off from the road about 3 m. out, and should be visited for the view of the channel and harbor. Portland Headlight is about a ¼ a mile off from the road, approached through a gateway, and by a path. The ocean view from the Light is worth seeing. Delano Park, about 4 miles out can be entered, although the bicyclist may have to dismount and walk one or two sharp rises. The Park is a picturesque place with many attractive features.

Almost to the Ocean House the Cape Lights ("Two Lights") may be reached by turning L., and this is a deviation from the route worth taking, for the opportunity it affords to see these light-houses and the life saving station near by.

The Shore Road gets into condition remarkably quick after bad weather, and is the most popular run out of Portland.

CAPE ELIZABETH AND SOUTH PORTLAND.

Cape Elizabeth, which was originally a part of ancient Falmouth, lies south of Portland, being separated from the city by the wide mouth of the Fore River, but connected in traffic and travel by ferries and a bridge.

The Cape, as it is familiarly called, contains about 13,000 acres of interesting territory. The original township was incorporated in 1765, and was first represented in General Court by James Leach. The clustered settlements lying upon the harbor opposite to Portland have borne the local names South Portland, Knightville, Turner's Island (other names being Point Village, "Ferry" Village and "Willard"), and the interior portion is settled by a farming population. The principal thoroughfares are the Cottage (Shore), Ocean House, Hannaford, Baren Hill, Fowler and Spurwink Roads, as will be seen by the accompanying map. Recently a division of the territory has been made, and the peninsula, if we may call it such, now consists of South Portland and Cape Elizabeth.

To the tourist perhaps the most remarkable feature of the Cape is its happy combination of rural scenery and ocean view, and the number of estates and villas occupying handsome sites on its bluffs and beaches. Wheelmen appreciate its good roads; for, though the way may be a trifle rolling, yet a ride with cool sea breezes (barring the vexatious head-wind) blending deliciously with the sweet smells of fields and wood — makes the alluring side-runs of Cape Elizabeth immensely attractive.

PORTLAND TO BUENA VISTA. — Leave Ocean House Road at signboard on R. at bend beyond crossing the "Shore" Road; or may be reached via Spurwink (see next page), but instead of keeping to R. toward Mitchell's, continue on over Grange Hill, as per frequent guide-boards. Distance 7 m., or about the same as to Mitchell's. This is southwestern point of the Cape, with a bold outlook. Good fishing.

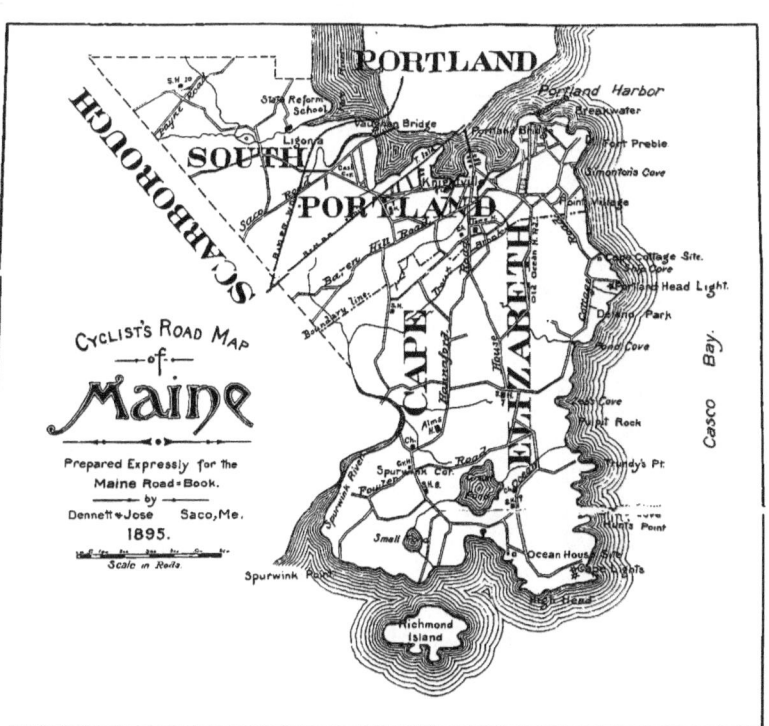

CAPE ELIZABETH RUNS.

PORTLAND TO SPURWINK according to Route No. 8 to Ocean House, only instead of turning last L. to Ocean House continue on Spurwink Road to Spurwink Meeting Honse, and from there to beach; in all about 2½ m. from the Ocean House.

Another route to Spurwink. Leave Portland by Vaughan Bridge, turning L. at Kerosene Works, after which it is a pretty straight road. This route leads to beyond Spurwink, but turn L. to Spurwink or R. to Prout's Neck passing Higgin's Beach; or take the Pleasant Hill road from Knightville, which is direct to the shore road, touching the same between Spurwink and Higgin's Beach.

HIGGINS' BEACH.—A short distance beyond Spurwink after crossing the river. Scarborough Beach is still further along the shore, while Prout's Neck is the terminus of the shore road, so called.

Another route to PROUT'S NECK is due west from Pond Cove schoolhouse. It is either first L. to Spurwink Meeting House, or R. for a short distance, then L. and generally straight on. Or from Knightville to Cape Elizabeth town house, then R. and continue straight on to shore road turning R. toward the Neck, 7 miles from Knightville.

HOTELS.—Mitchell's at Spurwink, The Kirkwood and Atlantic House at Scarborough Beach, and the Checkley House, L. A. W., Prout's Neck. Sea View Cottage, Pond Cove.

In fact, it will be seen that Cape Elizabeth is a network of roads, all of which average well for wheeling, and consequently the Cape is the most popular resort in the vicinity of Portland for the bicyclist.

"Hannaford's," near Pond Cove Schoolhouse, is where the boys often stop for refreshments in the shape of milk or eggs. Or a pole and line can be procured, and a mess of cunners hooked off the rocky shore not far from the road. The Veteran Cunner Association has a private house situated upon one of the projecting points of the shore about a mile beyond Pond Cove, and at the annual meetings held in August, some large fish stories are swapped among the members.

Indeed, it will be inferred that besides being a fine region for wheeling, the Cape is the place to visit for a jovial time generally.

PORTLAND TO WESTBROOK.

THROUGH ROUTE.   NO. 9.

SPECIFIC DIRECTIONS.	PASS THROUGH.	ROAD.	DISTANCE.
Preble House, R. Congress street, R., to Green, and over Deering Bridge and Forest avenue to Morrill's; here turn L. for Pride's Bridge.	Woodford's. Morrill's Corner. Pride's Bridge. *Westbrook.*	Generally good.	1½ Miles. 1¾ " 2¼ " 2¾ " 8 Miles.

[SPECIFIC DIRECTIONS CONTINUED].— After crossing same turn sharp L. and so on to Westbrook. Beyond Morrill's the highway is called the Windham Road. There is a new road to Cumberland Mills about 3 m. from Morrill's.

ANOTHER ROUTE TO WESTBROOK. (6 m.) — is to follow Congress street to State; turn R. to Deering Park ("The Oaks"); pass through Park bearing L. issuing upon Grove street; ascend hill and turn L. to Brighton Road, which continue straight to Westbrook, passing through Cumberland Mills. This route likely to be dusty, and road rough from heavy teaming. At Cumberland Mills is the largest paper-making concern in the country.

Or proceed to Woodfords following electric R. R.; turn L. still following track on Pleasant street, then L. again Stevens Plains Ave. to Spring, which take to Brighton Road; then continue as above. This is a way to the Presumpscot Trotting Park. Keep off sidewalks in Deering.

PORTLAND TO EVERGREEN CEMETERY. (3 m.) — Follow Electric R. R. track as in foregoing, but turn R. to Steven Plains Ave. which passes Cemetery gates.

PORTLAND TO COAL KILN CORNER. (6 m.) — Take reverse of Route No. 7 to Cash's Corner; bear R. and take first L. at Y.; proceed to meeting-house; swing sharply to R. and thence to destination.

ANOTHER WAY. — Through Stroudwater (see p. 25), and after crossing bridge and ascending hill keep to L. on a straight road. Public house — Larrabee's.

CYCLIST'S ROAD MAP
—of—
MAINE

Prepared Expressly for the
Maine Road-Book
—by—
Dennett & Jose   Saco, Me.
1895.

Scale in Miles

PORTLAND TO CORNISH.

Through Route.   No. 10.

Specific Directions.	Pass Through.	Road.	Distance.
Portland to Westbrook, like route via Brighton Road, page 22. Between Standish and Steep Falls, diverge from the old stage —	*Westbrook.* Gorham. West Gorham. Standish. *Cornish.*	Fair. Fair. Good. " Medium.	6 Miles. 4 " 2 " 4 " 14 " 30 Miles.

[SPECIFIC DIRECTIONS CONTINUED]. — Road (Route No. 13) and pass through Limington Bridge; then leave Limington Village to the left, and go through Ruin Corner to Cornish.

Cornish is a snug little village, with good stores and hotels. The bicycle repair shop of W. T. S. Morrison ought to be visited, likewise the Rooms of the Cornish Cycle Club in Jameson Block, where all touring wheelmen will be made welcome.

The above route is the most direct, but a more picturesque one can be had by going some 5 miles farther by way of Sebago Lake. Take Route No. 12, Portland to Sebago Lake (16 m.), thence to East Sebago (8 m.), thence to East Baldwin (4 m.), river road to Cornish Station (7 m.), stage road through Saco River Bridge to Cornish proper (1 m.). Total 36 m. Generally good roads.

HOTELS — Cornish, Lincoln House, L. A. W. $1.50.   PORTLAND, West End Hotel, $2.00.

PORTLAND TO BLACKSTRAP HILL.

Side Run   **No. 11.**

Specific Directions.	Pass Through.	Road.	Distance.
Start from Portland over Deering Bridge according to route No. 9.	Woodford's. Morrill's Corner. Allen's Corner. ***Blackstrap Hill.***	Fair, some hills.	$1\frac{3}{4}$ m. $1\frac{1}{4}$ " 1 " $4\frac{1}{2}$ "
			$8\frac{1}{2}$ m.

At Morrill's Corner turn R.; at Allen's Corner turn L. for a few rods, then take R. (Gray Road) for about a mile, and just beyond Frost's Woods turn L., and continue straight to Blackstrap Hill. Very steep hill other side of Presumpscot River, beyond covered bridge.

Another approach to BLACKSTRAP MONUMENT is to follow route No. 9 to Pride's Bridge, then continue straight, turning sharp R. at Pride's Corner, (5 m.), after which take first L. for back of Monument, or second L. for front. Blackstrap Hill is the highest elevation within fifty miles, and the Coast Survey has erected the monument thereon, which can be observed many miles out at sea.

FOR DUCK POND continue straight from Pride's Corner, 7 miles. A good place for lunch is at Mrs. Allen's, near junction of roads just beyond Monument where turn is made for Duck Pond. For a swim visit Duck Pond, but *walk*.

PORTLAND TO GOOSE POND (13 m.). — Note reference to Mrs. Allen's in above. Follow that direction to this point; then instead of turning L. as for Duck Pond, continue straight on for about 3 m., when turn L. at Mr. Copp's farm for the Pond, which is 1-2 m. in by logging road.

PORTLAND TO SEBAGO LAKE.

Side Run			No. 12.
Specific Directions.	Pass Through.	Road.	Distance.
To Westbrook same as Route via Brighton Rd. p. 22.	Woodfords. Cumberland Mills. ***Westbrook.*** South Windham. ***Sebago Lake.***	Fair.	6 Miles. 5 " 5 " 16 Miles.

The elevation of Sebago Lake is 267 feet above tide water; it is said to be over 400 feet in depth, and with its tributary lakelets has a superficial extent of more than 200 square miles. The Lake furnishes the water supply of the city of Portland, and in winter a product of ice. Its crystal water is not surpassed in the world for a city supply.

At L. from Westbrook take note of water pipes, and follow same to Lake. The better way to return is by way of Gorham, it being down grade and smoother road. There is a hotel at the Lake and splendid fishing and boating, as the length of this magnificent sheet of water is fourteen miles.

ANOTHER ROUTE TO WESTBROOK: Leave Preble House, continue upon Congress street up to and beyond the Union Station; then pass through Libby's Corner and Bradley Corner. Farther on at Stroudwater turn R. for Westbrook, which is about 5 m. from Union Station. Turn R. about a mile from Westbrook for Cumberland Mills.

PORTLAND TO FRYEBURG.

THROUGH ROUTE — No. 13.

SPECIFIC DIRECTIONS.	PASS THROUGH.	ROAD.	DISTANCE.
Portland to Westbrook, like Route via Brighton Road, p. 22. The better Road is via Cornish.	*Westbrook.*	Fair.	6 miles.
	Gorham.	not	4 "
	West Gorham.	particu-	2 "
	Standish.	larly	4 "
	Steep Falls.		6 "
	East Baldwin.	good.	2 "
	West Baldwin.	Good.	6 "
	Hiram.		5 "
	Brownfield.	Sandy.	7 "
	Fryeburg.		7 "
			49 Miles.

TO WHITE MOUNTAINS.—From Fryeburg to Lancaster, N. H., straight road by way of North Conway, Glen Station, by cars to Crawford House, then wheel to Fabyan House, then to Jefferson Hill and Lancaster,—in all about 70 miles from Portland.

A fine mountain trip is by train to Colebrook, N. H., then wheel from Colebrook over stage route direct to Bethel, Me., via. Dixville Notch, Errol, Upton, Grafton and Newry. Then from Bethel to Gorham, N. H., thence to Jefferson Heights; cross Cherry Mountain to the Twin Mountain House, then to Fabyan's, and from there to Crawford's and proceed down Crawford Notch to North Conway. The only piece of bad road in this whole tour is 20 miles, from Bethel to Gorham. This is an excellent trip being about all down grade, and through country noted for its wonderful scenery.

HOTEL.— FRYEBURG, Oxford House $.

PORTLAND TO BRIDGTON.

Side Run   **No. 14.**

Specific Directions.	Pass Through.	Road.	Distance.
Preble House, L. Congress street, L. Elm, L. Kennebec, across Deering Bridge, and so on same as Route 9; i. e. via Pride's Bridge.	Woodfords. Morrill's. Pride's Corner. Duck Pond. North Windham. Raymond. Naples. **Bridgton.**	Fair.	1¾ m. 1¼ " 2¼ " 2 " 7 " 5 " 12 " 8 "
			39½ m.

There is excellent fishing in Highland Lake near Bridgton. The Ridge, about a mile from Bridgton Center village, commands one of the finest views of the White Mountains that can be found on that side. Several boarding houses on the Ridge. Good fishing everywhere in this vicinity.

The tourist located at Bridgton can find Woods Pond, about 3 m. from the village, and hook bass in plenty. Moose Pond (4 m.) abounds in pickerel.

Pleasant side trips from Bridgton are : To Pleasant Mountain (7 m.) on the direct road to Fryeburg. To Waterford Flat (9 m.) via N. Bridgton (3 1-2 m.), Waterford City (8 m.) There are two ways, one under Bear Mt. on the east side of Bear Lake; the other on the west side of Bear Lake. Waterford Flat is the birthplace of Artemus Ward, and Waterford City his burial place. The roads here are excellent. The return trip can be made over the Ridge, which is good wheeling.

BRIDGTON TO SUMMIT SPRINGS, via N. Bridgton (3 1-2 m.) and Harrison (1 1-2 m.); thence to Summit Springs (3 m.) Go by way of Anonymous Pond, and return by Dawes' Hill. The bicyclist can ride to within half a mile of the Spring; then climb straight up. The view is very fine.

Some Cyclometer Distances of Side Runs Out of Portland.

Furnished by R. F. SAWYER.

Cape Elizabeth Ferry to Ocean House, via Shore Road, 7⅞ m. Return by Middle road 7 1-16 m.

To Morrill's Corner, via Shell Road, and return via Pleasant and Grove streets and Deering Oaks—8½ m.

To Yarmouth, via Falmouth Foreside; return by Upper road—25½ m.

To Atlantic House, Scarborough Beach, via Vaughan Bridge; return Hannaford and Middle roads and Ferry—21⅛ m.

To Atlantic House, by Cape Elizabeth town-house; return Hannaford and Middle Roads and Knightville—22 6-8 m.

To Blackstrap, through Oaks, Grove street and Shell Road to Pride's Bridge, then R. round base of Hill—11⅜ m. Return via Duck Pond and Windham Road—10½ m.

Cape Cottage, up "Royer's Hill"; return Sawyer street—6⅞ m.

To Blackstrap, via Shell Road and Ocean street, turn L. to Allen's Corner, and on through Covered Bridge, turning R. and L. beyond; return via Piscataqua Corner, Falmouth, Smelt Hill, Morrill's and Woodford's—26¼ m.

To Old Orchard, via Dunstan's Corner, Pine Point and Beach and return—34 m. (Think this must include 3 or 4 m. riding at Beach.)

To Spurwink, Bowery Beach,—11 m. plus.

To Prout's Neck, Hannaford Road; return Ocean House—30¼ m.

To Prout's Neck, via Middle Road; return Shore Road—26¼ m.

Cape Elizabeth Ferry to Prout's Neck, by Shore and Hannaford Roads—13 m.

Portland to Prout's Neck by way of Oak Hill—12½ m.

To Harpswell, through Falmouth Foreside to Yarmouth—41⅓ m.

To Prout's Neck, via Shore and Hannaford Roads; return via "Mitchell's," Town House and Ferry—25¼ m.

To Old Orchard, Saco and Biddeford—40¾ m. (Think this includes 3 or 4 m. riding about Saco and Biddeford.)

To Kennebunk, via Saco and Biddeford—28⅞ m.

To Higgin's Beach and Prout's Neck by town-house; return Oak Hill—25 m.

To Biddeford Pool, via Saco and Biddeford; return same—47¾ m.

To Gray, via Oaks, Grove street, Forest Avenue and Gray Road—17½ m. Return via Blackstrap and Allens Corner—18⅝ m.

To "Hannaford's," near Pond Cove Schoolhouse, by way of Ferry and Shore Road; return Middle Road and Ferry—12¾ m.

To Kirkwood House, Scarborough Beach, via Ferry and Hannaford Road; return Oak Hill—25½ m.

To Gorham, by way of Saccarappa; returning J. B. Curtis and Congress street—23⅝ m.

To Pine Point, via Saco Road: return Old Orchard, Saco and Biddeford—38⅓ m.

To Smelt Hill, West Falmouth, and Pride's Bridge—18¾ m.

To Prout's Neck, via Oak Hill; return via Bowery Beach and Shore Road—29 m.

To Walnut Hill, through Oaks, Woodford's and Lunt's Corners and Cumberland Center—17 m. Return through Yarmouth and Upper Road (or Middle) to Cumberland, turn L. to Falmouth Foreside Road—16⅝ m.

To Ocean House, via Oak Hill; return by way of shore road—24 m.

To Saco over Scottin's Hill; return Saco Road—33 m.

To Presumpscot Falls, via Washington street; return the same—11⅝ m.

To Kirkwood House, Scarborough Beach, via Ferry and Shore Road, to woods beyond Mt. Misery, then right hand road bearing R.; return via Spurwink Road to town-house and ferry—22⅕ m.

To Old Orchard, a pretty ride is to turn L. from Saco road before getting to Old Orchard direct road. Round trip 31¼ m.

The above furnish valuable suggestions for bicycling around Portland.

PORTLAND TO WESCUSTIGO SPRING.

SIDE RUN　　　　　(WALNUT HILL.)　　　　　No. 15.

Specific Directions.	Pass Through.	Road.	Distance.
Preble House, L. Congress street, L. to Washington, then Tukey's Bridge straight on through East Deering to Allen's Corner, then Gray Road to Cumberland, and there diverge to Walnut Hill.	East Deering. Lunt's Corner. Allen's Corner. West Falmouth. Cumberland Center. Walnut Hill and *Wescustigo Spring.*	Good. Fair.	1¾ Miles. 1 " 3½ " 5 " 8 "
			20 Miles.

Hotel at Spring—Wescustigo House. For variety return by way of Yarmouth and Shore Road to Portland. 16 miles.

YARMOUTH TO POWNAL.—7 m., and thence to Gray Road, which join at New Gloucester. Yarmouth to Portland clay road much broken up by heavy granite teams.

PORTLAND TO WALNUT HILL.—A more direct route would be via Colley's Corner, (for which turn R. at Lunt's Corner, and proceed 3¾ m.); then turn L. at Y. for Cumberland, and proceed through Cumberland Center to Walnut Hill. Distance about 14 miles.

PORTLAND TO BATH.—via Orr's Island. Take Harpswell steamer to Orr's Island, then proceed across that Island (4 m.) and by bridge to Great Island (5 m.) crossing another bridge (at Gurnet) to mainland; thence 9 m. to Bath. See also Routes Nos. 16 and 25.

PORTLAND TO BRUNSWICK.

THROUGH ROUTE — **NO. 16.**

Specific Directions.	Pass Through.	Road.	Distance.
Preble House, Congress L., Washington street L., Tukey's Bridge to East Deering, then R. Veranda street, past Marine Hospital, over Martin's Bridge, and straight road through—	Falmouth Foreside. Cumberland. Yarmouth. Freeport. *Brunswick.*	Fair. Yarmouth to Freeport clay road. Sandy near Brunswick.	7 Miles. 3 " 1 " 6 " 8 "
			25 Miles.

[SPECIFIC DIRECTIONS CONTINUED]. — Falmouth Foreside and Cumberland, following telegraph poles.

PORTLAND TO YARMOUTH. — About 10 m. by shore road; 15 m. by "upper road" through Falmouth and Cumberland. Former the better road. The Underwood Spring may be found at Falmouth Foreside; take path at R. just beyond sign "Casco Terrace." New Summer Club-house of P. W. C. members near Town Landing.

YARMOUTH TO FREEPORT (6 m.) direct road. Just over the bridge turn R. for South Freeport, which is the preferable route on account of road and scenery. FREEPORT, Hotel Harlow, $2.00; Gem Cottage, dinner $.50.

YARMOUTH TO PRINCE'S POINT — Main street east via Pleasant, fair road (3 m.). YARMOUTH, Royal River House, $1.75, 50 cents per meal.

BRUNSWICK TO MARE POINT, (7 m. south). First two miles sandy. Generally sandy in neighborhood of Brunswick, but wheelmen have fixed several side-paths. HOTEL. — City Hotel, $1.00. No side-walk riding permitted.

BRUNSWICK TO HARPSWELL. — Tontine Hotel, Main street to Cong. church; back of church take R. road by college buildings, and continue for ½ m. Take R. at Y. for Harpswell, as L. leads to Orr's and Great Islands. This route passes through N. Harpswell, Harpswell Center, So. Harpswell to Potts Point (15 m.). The roads to Orr's Island (14 m.) and Cundy's Harbor are hard. Merriconeag House $. Points of interest from Brunswick: New Wharf (4 m.), Gurnet House at Gurnet Bridge (5 m.). Portland to Harpswell this route.

PORTLAND TO AUBURN AND LEWISTON.

Through Route (VIA GRAY AND DANVILLE JUNCTION.) **No 17.**

Specific Directions.	Pass Through.	Road.	Distance.
See Route No. 15, Portland to Gray Road; then pass through West Falmouth and West Cumberland to Gray.	Gray. New Gloucester. Danville Junction. *Auburn. Lewiston.*	Fair. Sandy.	16 Miles. 6 " 5 " 6½ " 1½ "
			35 Miles.

POLAND SPRING 5 miles from Danville Junction by a picturesque route. Side run, Gray to Dry Mills, (3 m.) to the Pavilion at Dry Pond.

GRAY.—Hotel Parker, dinner 50 cts.

AUBURN.—Elm House, Court street, $2.00. LEWISTON, DeWitt House, L. A. W., Pine street, $2.00. Bicycle club at Lewiston, Lewiston and Auburn Bicycle Club. Take note of Falls in Androscoggin River; good view from bridge between Lewiston and Auburn.

AUBURN TO LAKE AUBURN, Side-run 3 miles, by way of Turner and Center streets, fair road, following street-car track. At Lake is good boating and fishing. Steamer "Lewiston" makes regular trips. About ½ mile from Grove is Mt. Gile, where there is an observatory. A fine view may be had.

PORTLAND TO RANGELEY LAKES can be accomplished by way of Auburn, South Paris, and Bryant's Pond. See Routes Nos. 21, 23 and 24.

BRUNSWICK TO AUGUSTA.

THROUGH ROUTE   No. 18.

Specific Directions.	Pass Through.	Road.	Distance.
Main street, cross bridge to Topsham, then R., following river in dry weather; but after heavy rains better to follow road bordered by telegraph poles. It is farther from Brunswick to Bowdoinham by way of river, but less sand.	Topsham. Bowdoinham. Richmond. Gardiner. Hallowell. *Augusta.*	Good. Few hills not rideable. Generally good; some bad hills.	1 Mile. 9 " 7 " 10 " 4 " 2 " 33 Miles.

RICHMOND TO GARDINER take "Meadow Road." Make inquiries, as road is confusing sometimes. West side of river the better road.

GARDINER TO AUGUSTA, follow wires. Many steep hills. This route will pass through the beautiful town of Farmingdale, then level road for 2 miles; further on Louden Hill, hard climb, but safe coast. Then Steam Mill Hill which do not coast, as there is railroad crossing at bottom. When in sight of State House, Augusta, prepare for a grand coast.

GARDINER TO TOGUS, 5 miles east, over Gardiner and Randolph Bridge, turn L. about 1 mile out, and take northeasterly course to Togus. At Chelsea corner (2½ m.) turn L. This is better than the straight road.

FROM TOGUS TO AUGUSTA (4 m.); very fine road through Togus, though hilly near Augusta. Coasting these hills not recommended, though ventured by local riders. National Soldiers Home located at Togus, where there are about 1700 soldiers.

HOTELS — BOWDOINHAM, Stimson Hotel, $1.50. GARDINER, Evans House, $1.50. HALLOWELL, Hallowell House, $2.00. AUGUSTA, Augusta House, $2.00. RICHMOND, Richmond Hotel, $1.25.

LEWISTON TO BRUNSWICK.

THROUGH ROUTE   **No. 19.**

SPECIFIC DIRECTIONS.	PASS THROUGH.	ROAD.	DISTANCE.
DeWitt House, Pine street R., Lisbon street L., straight on through Lisbon to Lisbon Falls. At Lisbon Falls bear to R., and take river road.	Lisbon. Lisbon Falls. *Brunswick.*	Pretty hilly. Sandy near Brunswick.	6 Miles. 3 " 9 " 18 Miles.

Generally poor road. Worst between Lisbon Fall and Brunswick. About 2 miles of coal-ash sidewalk between Lisbon and Lisbon Falls which should be taken advantage of.

LISBON FALLS TO FREEPORT, (8 m.) Cross railroad, turn L. then cross river and turn L. for Freeport. Generally good road. HOTEL, LISBON FALLS, ME. Central House, $2.00.

BRUNSWICK. A very pretty town, the seat of Bowdoin College, where have graduated by far the most of the notable statesmen of Maine. It is worth one's while to walk through the College grounds, visit the Chapel to view the paintings; also the Library, where some fine statuary is exhibited.

The Bowdoin Paper Co. is one of the lively industries of the place, having an output of about 20 tons per day. The river is crossed by a fine iron bridge and the arrangements for water power make a fine sight. Sidewalk riding prohibited. Go in swimming at Diving Rock.

LEWISTON TO AUGUSTA.

THROUGH ROUTE (VIA WINTHROP.) **No. 20.**

SPECIFIC DIRECTIONS.	PASS THROUGH.	ROAD.	DISTANCE.
Leave by way of Sabattus street. Within one-half mile of Sabattus cross M. C. R. R. and turn to L., which fetches rioer into Market Square, Sabattus. Turn R., cross—	Sabattus. Monmouth. *Winthrop.* Manchester. *Augusta.*	Good. Some hills. Hilly.	6 Miles. 10 " 6 " 8 " 4½ "
			34½ Miles.

[SPECIFIC DIRECTIONS CONTINUED.] M. C. R. R., then L. by Sabattus Pond, and first L. straight to Monmouth. Only chance for missing the road is a Y half way from Sabattus to Monmouth, at foot of steep hill. Bear to L. here.

Keep straight on through Monmouth Center, across railroad track, to North Monmouth. About 2 miles from Monmouth Center, straight road to Winthrop. From Sabattus to Monmouth is best stretch of road in Androscoggin county; it follows shore of Sabattus Pond for several miles, and the scenery is " enchanting."

WINTHROP TO AUGUSTA.—A straight and direct stage road with some hills. Augusta is the capital of Maine. It is prettily situated, and the state house is a point of interest On account of many hills it is not a favorable place for bicycling.

LEWISTON TO BRYANT'S POND, about 50 miles, along Androscoggin River, passing through Keene's Mills (12½ m.), North Turner (5 m.), Brettun's Mills (3 m.), Canton Village (5 m.), Dixfield (10 m.), and Rumford Falls (10 m.) Very good road, and through many picturesque places.

HOTELS—MONMOUTH, Monmouth House, $2.00. WINTHROP, Winthrop House, $2.00.

LEWISTON SIDE-RUNS.

LEWISTON TO TURNER. — Take Main street to Barkerville, then turn L. on what is known as Switzerland or River Road. Two miles out from Lewiston the fair ground is passed, where the annual exhibition of the Maine State Association is held. Continue North, and at a distance of 12 m. cross the river over the new iron bridge (formerly a ferry); thereafter ride due West to Turner Centre (3½ m.), and thence to Turner village by direct road.

To RETURN, turn L. at Turner Centre on Turner lower street, and continue direct to Auburn, passing Lake Auburn and traversing what would be the hypotenuse of the triangle, considering that geometrical figure as illustrating the round trip. Whole distance (cyclometer) 29 m. Road sandy, but generally fair. If tourist wishes to get to Turner by shortest route, reverse above and leave Auburn as per run "Around Lake Auburn." Ten miles to Turner this way. Road good, but hilly.

LEWISTON TO SABATTUS POND. — Leave city same as by route No. 20 to Sabattus, at which point turn L. at drug store, making all turns to the right until shore of pond is passed, and a high hill climbed. At top of hill take right at Y. One mile beyond turn L. and follow travelled road to Green Depot. Then return to Lewiston either via College or Main streets.

AROUND LAKE AUBURN. — Follow electric road out of Auburn to Lake Grove; then proceeding, follow shore, making all turns L. Whole run about 15 m., reckoning from the Court House. The best short run out of Lewiston.

LEWISTON TO COBBOSSEECONTEE POND. — Leave city according to route No. 20 to Sabattus village. Turn right at drug store, cross Maine Central R. R., take first L., which leads to Day's Corner. Here turn square L. and about ¼ m. farther on turn R. Continue about 4 m., and turn R. again at schoolhouse, then immediately turn to L. to shore of pond. Good bass fishing. Hammond's Grove at north end of pond, — great summer resort for Augusta people.

LEWISTON SIDE-RUNS. — (*Continued.*)

TO RETURN. At schoolhouse strike across the country 4 m. to Monmouth Centre, then continue according to route No. 20, or according to the new route to Augusta given below.

LEWISTON TO AUGUSTA. (ANOTHER ROUTE.) Leave Lewiston on either Main or College streets, which take the bicyclist to Green Depot. College road the better in dry weather, being clay surface. This route passes through Green Depot (7½ m.). The same distance (7½ m.) farther on a turn in the road may be taken right to Monmouth Centre. Continue direct to North Monmouth, from which place it is 3¼ m. to Winthrop, and thence 10 m. to Augusta. Whole distance 30 m., straight road throughout. The road to Winthrop, though somewhat hilly, is the best one out of Lewiston.

Every member of the L. A. W. (in fact, every wheelman) should be unceasing in his agitation for better roads. Not only are good roads important for wheeling, but they mark the progress of civilization.

It is not an uncommon sight abroad to observe the road inspector with a small ring of iron in his hand, and every stone picked up that will not pass through the ring is thrown in a pile by the roadside to be broken into fragments. This may be regarded as scrupulous care of roads. Does it pay? Undoubtedly it does; otherwise the governments of a world old in experience would not look after the matter so carefully. Gen. Q. A. Gilmore proved by experiments that any one of the better class of permanent roadways would enable a team to draw on a level about four times the amount drawn on a common dirt road; and Clements Herschel, the civil engineer, has said that on the roads of England a horse can perform twice the work the same animal could accomplish in America.

Taking the Pennsylvania-Maryland-New Jersey-and-Delaware Road Book, which is comprised within one cover, in connection with this volume, the tourist will have directions practically covering the riding districts of the Eastern States, namely, Maine, Massachusetts, Vermont, Connecticut, Rhode Island, New York, New Jersey, Delaware, Maryland, District of Columbia, Pennsylvania, Virginia, Ohio, Illinois, and Missouri. L. A. W. members can buy this book for $1. Regular price $1.50.

LEWISTON TO MECHANIC FALLS.

THROUGH ROUTE.

No. 21.

Specific Directions.	Pass Through.	Road.	Distance.
Lisbon street. Turn L., crossing Main street bridge to Auburn. Leave that city by Minot avenue direct to Minot corner. Turn square R. at grocery store, and —	*Auburn.* Minot Corner. *Mechanic Falls.*	Some sand, but generally good.	6 Miles. 4 " 10 Miles.

[SPECIFIC DIRECTIONS CONTINUED.] — Take first L., crossing stream and immediately turning R. Direct road then to Mechanic Falls. The Hebron road will be noted on right 2 m. from Auburn.

AUBURN TO NORWAY (22 m.). — Leave Auburn by Minot Ave.; continue 2 m. on this thoroughfare, then turn R. for Hebron road. From this turn proceed to West Minot (10 m.); then pass through Hebron (3 m.), South Paris (5 m.), Norway (2 m.). This route to Norway is considered by some as better than through Mechanic Falls.

MECHANIC FALLS TO CANTON (26 m.); through West Minot, Buckfield (14 m.), East Sumner and Hartford Centre. Not a first-class road. The Androscoggin River is reached a few miles north of Canton (at Canton Point), where connection can be made with road to Dixfield, or to Livermore Falls.

LIVERMORE FALLS TO FARMINGTON. — Through North Jay and East Wilton. Good road.

HOTELS — LEWISTON, Exchange, $1.50. NORWAY, Beale House, $1.50. Keep off the sidewalks in these places.

MECHANIC FALLS TO FRYEBURG.

THROUGH ROUTE (VIA BRIDGTON.) **No. 22.**

Specific Directions.	Pass Through.	Road.	Distance.
Pleasant Street north; follow telegraph poles.	Welchville. Norway. *Harrison.* North Bridgton. Bridgton. *Fryeburg.*	Sandy. Fair. Good.	4 Miles. 6 " 12 " 1½ " 3½ " 14 "
			41 Miles.

NORTH BRIDGTON TO FRYEBURG, another route, is by way of Waterford and Lovell (15 miles.) Rather a round-about way and hilly, but the surface of the road is hard and firm.

FRYEBURG TO BETHEL HILL by way of Lovell Village, Lovell No. 4, Lovell Centre, North Lovell, East Stoneham and North Waterford, about 20 miles, and somewhat hilly. At Fryeburg is held the annual camp meeting at Martha's Grove, and considerable religious enthusiasm there prevails. This part of Maine, just over the border from Starr Kings, "White Hills" of New Hampshire, and contiguous to the lake region of the Bridgtons, is a rare trysting place for the summer tourist, and the sportsman finds there entertainment a great deal to his liking.

HOTELS— BRIGHTON, Bridgton House, $1.50. FRYEBURG, Fryeburg House and Walker House, $1.50.

MECHANIC FALLS TO BETHEL HILL.

THROUGH ROUTE NO. 23.

SPECIFIC DIRECTIONS.	PASS THROUGH.	ROAD.	DISTANCE.
Follow line Grand Trunk Railway. Cross iron bridge, turn R., then L up hill, crossing R. F. & B, R. R., then L. to Welchville. Leave Welchville via Oxford Plains.	Welchville. *South Paris.* West Paris. *Bryant's Pond.* Locke's Mills. Walker's Mills. *Bethel Hill.*	Somewhat hilly, but not bad.	4 Mile. 7 " 8¼ " 6 " 4 " 4 " 2 "
			35½ Miles.

Between South Paris and West Paris, Snow's Falls is passed. Then beyond, at junction of roads, take L. for Bryant's Pond. At Bryant's Pond bear L. after passing Grand Trunk R. R. station, then straight road, crossing bridge, and L. to Locke's Mills. Or turn R. at Trap Corner (beyond Snow's Falls) and thus secure a better road by going perhaps a mile farther.

BETHEL TO RUMFORD FALLS (23 m.) — Via Newry, following north bank of river the whole way. Pretty run through fine scenery.

BETHEL HILL TO RANGELY LAKES (28 m.), by way of Newry Corner; then follow river to Grafton; thence to Upton and shore of Umbagog Lake. This route is not so good as from Bryant's Pond.

BETHEL HILL TO BRIDGTON CENTRE (about 21 m.); through North Waterford, Waterford Flat, Waterford City and North Bridgton by way of Waterford road. For 10 miles quite sandy.

HOTELS. — SOUTH PARIS, Andrews House, $1.50. BETHEL HILL, Bethel House, $1.00. BRYANT'S POND, Glen Mountain House, $

40

BRYANT'S POND TO RANGELEY LAKES.

THROUGH ROUTE   **No. 24.**

SPECIFIC DIRECTIONS.	PASS THROUGH.	ROAD.	DISTANCE.
Through North Woodstock, Milton, Rumford Corner, Rumford Point, North Rumford, South Andover; cross Androscoggin River—	Milton. Rumford. Andover. To South arm of Lake.	Good.	4 miles. 2 " 15 " 12 " 33 Miles.

[SPECIFIC DIRECTIONS CONTINUED].—At Rumford Point, and Ellis River about half a mile above.
At Andover turn east again across Ellis River, following Byron road 2½ m., then turn N. W., and guide-boards will direct by straight road to south arm of Richardson Lakes.
Or turn west at Andover toward Upton (16m.), which will bring rider to shores of Umbagog Lake. This latter road is rough, and has one hill 4½ m. long.
Or continue from Bethel toward Rangeley Lakes through Gilead, Shelburne, and Gorham, N.H.; then north to Berlin Falls, Milan and Errol, where take the steamer for any part of Rangeley Lakes. Through Berlin, Milan Corner, and Dummer to Errol there is 35 m. of as good riding as can be found in Maine.

BRYANT'S POND TO DIXFIELD: to Milton (3 m.). Cross ferry just before entering Rumford Centre (6 m.), and proceed on east side of river until new (free) bridge is reached, which cross and pass through Rumford Falls (5 m.). Leave Rumford Falls, crossing new (toll) bridge, which issues upon the other side at Ridlonville, not far from Mexico; from thence proceed (4 m.) to Dixfield.

DIXFIELD TO WELD LAKE.—A pretty run of 12 m. via Berry's Mills (7 m.). Hotels at lake if one would stop for trout or salmon fishing. Mt. Blue, the greatest elevation in this region, not far distant.

BRUNSWICK TO ROCKLAND.

Through Route (VIA BATH.) **No. 25.**

Specific Directions.	Pass Through.	Road.	Distance.
Tontine House, Main street, and cross bridge to Topsham (1 m.) Follow river to Bay Bridge, which cross, and proceed until telegraph poles appear, which follow to Bath. Fine view of Merry Meeting Bay from Bay Bridge.	*Bath.* Woolwich. Wiscasset. Damariscotta. Waldoboro. Warren. Thomaston. *Rockland.*	Level 6 m. Balance hilly. Hilly. and rough.	10 Miles. 2 " 10 " 9 " 10 " 7 " 5 " 4 "
			57 Miles.

[SPECIFIC DIRECTIONS CONTINUED.]—Or go by way of Brunswick road (9 m.), which is not so good traveling. On this route take left road at Y, 3 miles from Brunswick, then be guided by telegraph poles.

From **WOOLWICH** direct road to Rockland. Roads rideable, but with some bad places. Perhaps worst in vicinity of Waldoboro, but wheelmen are alive to the need for better highways, and improvements will come.

Between Topsham and Bath is Ham's Hill, commonly considered a hard ride. On this hill, near windmill, turn sharp R. for Adams House, on New Meadows River (5 m. from Brunswick), a place formerly famous for fish dinners.

WALDOBORO TO BELFAST (30 m.)—via Union (10 m.), Appleton (5 m.), Searsmont (5 m.), Belfast (10 m.). Better road, and more direct than by way of Rockland. (See Route No. 37.)

HOTELS — WISCASSET, Hilton House, $1.50; DAMARISCOTTA, Main Hotel, $2.00; WALDOBORO, Riverside Hotel, $1.50; THOMASTON, Knox House, $2.00; ROCKLAND, Thorndike House, $2.50.

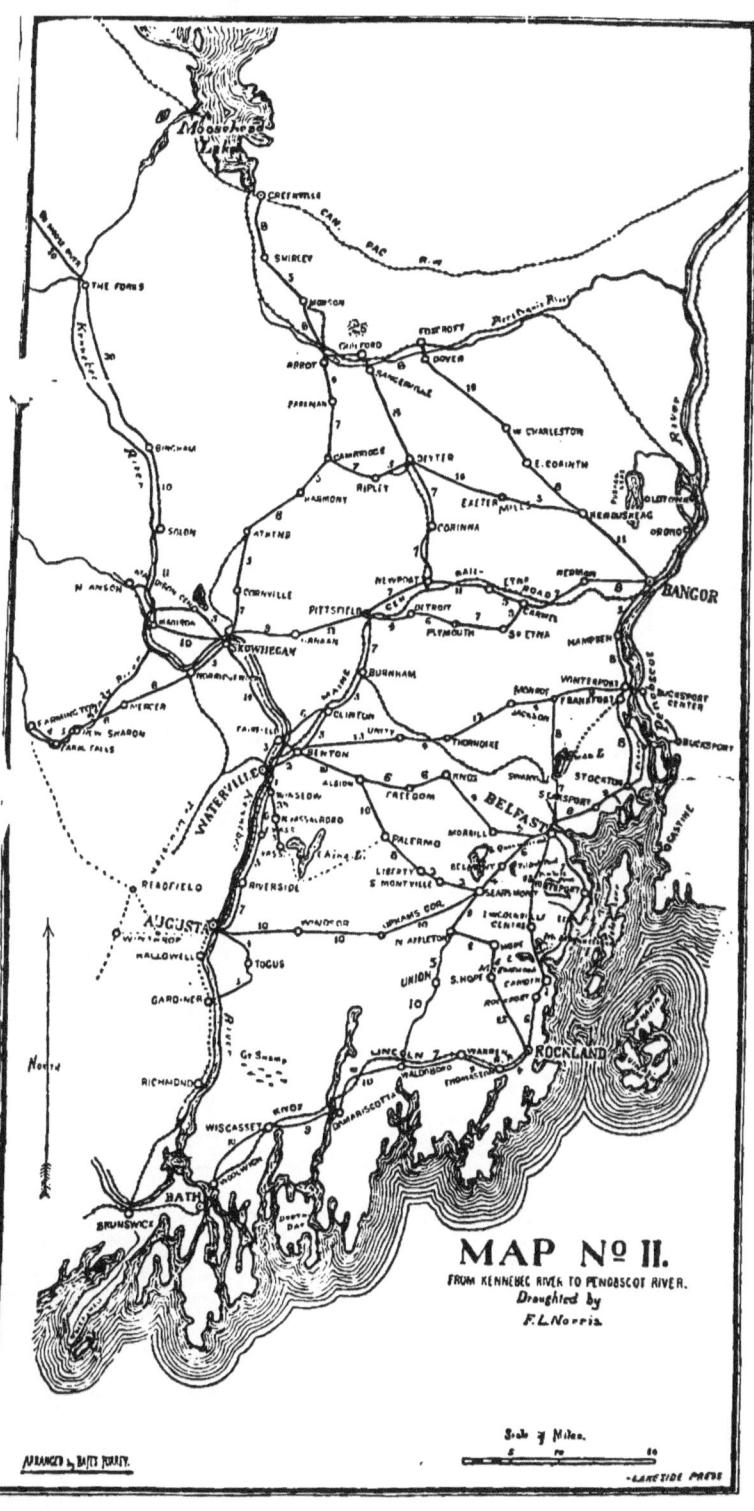

AUGUSTA TO BELFAST.

THROUGH ROUTE   **NO. 26.**

SPECIFIC DIRECTIONS.	PASS THROUGH.	ROAD.	DISTANCE.
Coney House, Water street, R. to Bridge street, then cross river. Proceed by Lincoln street L. to Bangor, and R. to Belfast road.	Windsor. Upham's Corner. *Searsmont.* Belmont Corner. *Belfast.*	Rough, and through woods. Very fair. Not so good. Good.	10 Miles. 10 " 10 " 4 " 6 " —— 40 Miles.

[SPECIFIC DIRECTIONS CONTINUED.]—Bear L. to Upham's Corner; also L. to Searsmont, and R. to Belmont; thence to Belfast. ☞ After Upham's Cor. pass through Somerville and So. Liberty.

Quantabacook Pond, near Searsmont, good fishing and swimming. Tilden's Pond, 6 miles from Belfast, is famous for white perch, pickerel, and duck shooting.

This route was formerly an old stage road, and every 5 miles there was an inn where the wayfarer stopped for refreshments—more liquid, perhaps, than obtains to-day. Heavy brass knockers on the doors, and fireplaces that would hold a stick of wood 3½ feet long, were common in those days.

AUGUSTA TO TOGUS—Leave Coney House, cross bridge, then R. at top of hill to Coney street; proceed half a mile, then L. and direct to Togus. Latter place notable for flower-beds and well-kept grounds. Open air band concert every Sunday afternoon in summer.

AUGUSTA TO WINTHROP—From Coney House south, up Rines' Hill to Grove street, cross State to Western Avenue, then direct to Winthrop; this is one way toward Farmington.

HOTELS—BELFAST, Crosby Inn, L. A. W., $2.00; and Phœnix House $1.50.

AUGUSTA TO SKOWHEGAN.

THROUGH ROUTE (VIA WATERVILLE.) **No. 27.**

SPECIFIC DIRECTIONS.	PASS THROUGH.	ROAD.	DISTANCE.
Start Coney House, Water street L. over bridge, R. up Coney to Bangor street; then L. and straight road, crossing Kennebec at Winslow into Waterville.	Riverside. Vassalboro. Winslow. *Waterville.* Fairfield. *Skowhegan.*	Hilly and some sand. Good road beyond Vassalboro; ½ mile sand, then fair.	7 Miles. 5 " 5 " 1 " 2 " 15 "
			35 Miles.

ANOTHER WAY.—Take L. bank Kennebec River via Sidney, reached by crossing ferry at Vassalboro R. R. station; then direct to Waterville.

WATERVILLE TO FAIRFIELD via College street, first-class road.

FAIRFIELD TO SKOWHEGAN—One route via Main street, Shawmut and Pishon's Ferry, sandy road; another, L. to Western Avenue and Fairfield Centre; hilly, but fine scenery.

There is a fine side-run from Winslow (7 m.), through North Vassalboro to East Vassalboro, near China Pond. Hotel, Bradley's—favorite run from Waterville.—good fishing Old Fort Halifax is also at Winslow, near bridge.

AUGUSTA TO FARMINGTON—One route is to pass through Manchester, Readfield, Mt. Vernon, Vienna, and Farmington Falls—about 30 miles.

HOTELS — WATERVILLE, Elmwood Hotel, L. A. W., $2.00. SKOWHEGAN, Hotel Coburn, L. A. W., $1.50. FAIRFIELD, Fairfield House $1.40.

AUGUSTA TO ROCKLAND.

Through Route — No. 28.

Specific Directions.	Pass Through.	Road.	Distance.
Same as Route No. 26 to Searsmont, then southeast to North Appleton. From Hope to Rockland this route passes through Rockville and West Camden.	Windsor. Upham's Corner. *Searsmont.* North Appleton. Hope. South Hope. *Rockland.*		30 Miles. 4 " 4 " 5 " 12 "
			55 Miles.

HOTELS—SEARSMONT, Nevins House, $1.50.

WATERVILLE TO ROCKLAND.

Through Route — No. 29.

Specific Directions.	Pass Through.	Road.	Distance.
Elmwood Hotel, College street to Fairfield, then Main street R. to bridge, and across Kennebec to Benton. From Searsmont southeast same as route No. 28.	Benton. Albion. Palermo. Liberty. South Montville. Searsmont. *Rockland.*		3 Miles. 10 " 8 " 8 " 2 " 4 " 25 "
			60 Miles.

OR, REVERSE,— Thomaston (4 m.), Warren (8 m.), Jefferson (12 m.), Windsor (Four Corners) and East Vassalboro — total 54 miles.

WATERVILLE TO BELFAST.

Through Route No. 30.

Specific Directions.	Pass Through.	Road.	Distance.
Elmwood, corner Main and College streets. Take straight road (College St.) to Fairfield, where bear to R. and cross river to Benton; then direct road and L. to Freedom, R. to Knox, L. to Morrill school-house, R. to Poor's Mills, down hill L. to Belfast, by Trotting Park through Belmont avenue to city. This is stage route. Look out for a bad hill in Knox.	Benton. Albion. Freedom. Foster's Corner. Knox. Morrill. Poor's Mills. *Belfast.*	Some hills, which can be ridden with ease. Fine road.	3 miles. 10 " 6 " 6 " 3 " 2 " 5 " —— 35 Miles.

Hotels—Sparrow's Tavern at Freedom, $. C. Wellington's at Albion, $

WATERVILLE TO WINTERPORT.

Through Route No. 31.

Specific Directions.	Pass Through.	Road.	Distance.
Same as No. 30 to Benton, then east to Unity. At Monroe Village turn south for Belfast (15 m.) At Winterport cross Penobscot River to Bucksport Centre, and continue to Ellsworth, if desired, via Bucksport and Orland.	Benton. Unity. Thorndike. Jackson. Monroe Village. *Winterport.*	Hard road.	3 Miles. 13 " 4 " 12 " 4 " 9 " —— 45 Miles.

Hotels—Winterport, Commercial Hotel, $1.50. Unity, Central Hotel, $1.50.

WATERVILLE TO MOOSEHEAD LAKE.

THROUGH ROUTE (VIA PITTSFIELD.) **No 32.**

SPECIFIC DIRECTIONS.	PASS THROUGH.	ROAD.	DISTANCE.
Waterville to Fairfield via College St. Leave Fairfield, Main street to bridge. Cross river and then bear L. into Benton. Proceed through Clinton up long hill, keeping to L., then straight road to Burnham.	*Fairfield.* Benton. Clinton. Burnham. *Pittsfield.* Newport. Corinna. *Dexter.* Sangerville. Guilford. Abbot. Monson. Shirley. *Greenville.*	A very good run. Generally good.	2 Miles. 3 " 4 " 5 " 7 " 7 " 7 " 7 " 8¼ " 11 " 3 " 9 " 7 " 7 "
			78 Miles.

[SPECIFIC DIRECTIONS CONTINUED.]—This is the sportsman's route to the Lake, which is the region for fishing and hunting. Trout will be found plentiful in the Churchill stream.

DEXTER TO CAMBRIDGE, (12 m.), via Ripley (5 m.), take new road just out of Dexter to avoid bad hill. This connects with route No. 35.

HOTELS—CLINTON, Clinton House, $1.50. DEXTER, Exchange Hotel, $2.00. GREENVILLE, Moosehead Lake Inn, $. MT. KINEO, Kineo House,—twenty miles up the Lake; take steamer at Greenville Junction.

SKOWHEGAN TO FARMINGTON.

THROUGH ROUTE **No. 33.**

Specific Directions.	Pass Through.	Road.	Distance.
Hazelton House, Water street, L. to Madison, then L. to Elm, leaving town via Elm and following river.	*Norridgewock.* Mercer. New Sharon. Farmington Falls. *Farmington.*	Good.	5 Miles. 8 " 6 " 5 " 4 " 28 Miles.

Road generally good, with gravel bottom, and few sandy places. Grade easy. One can ride to Mercer (13 m.) without dismounting.

SKOWHEGAN TO MADISON ("HAYDEN") LAKE.—Madison street first L, after crossing small stream one-half mile from town, then direct road (5½m.), through Madison Centre. At Madison there is the largest pulp mill in Maine.

FARMINGTON TO DIXFIELD (25 m.); through East Wilton, Wilton, and East Dixfield. Road sandy part of the way, with some hills; but generally quite good.

FARMINGTON TO STRONG.—The road is good on the left bank of the river. From Strong to Phillips the better road is on the right bank; north to Kingfield it is also first-class wheeling.

HOTELS.—NORRIDGEWOCK, Sawyer House, $1.50. FARMINGTON, Elm House, $2.00.

SKOWHEGAN SIDE-RUNS.

SKOWHEGAN TO OLD POINT MONUMENT (Madison). (12 m.) — Hotel Coburn, Elm street, and direct road to within ¼ m. of Norridgewock; here bear to R. instead of following road alongside river, take first L. a little farther on, which immediately turns R. and through Norridgewock, (5 m.) and up the hill and out of town above bridge. Thence to Old Point (7 m.), which must be closely watched for at L. of highway. Cross on monument placed there at expense of Skowhegan Wheel Club, who discovered original one where it had fallen after storms and frost of winter of 1890. Fine spring of mineral water on river bank a short distance above monument. Village of Madison Bridge 1½ m. up the river.

SKOWHEGAN TO LAKE GEORGE (8 m.). — Hotel Coburn, Russell street to Water. Proceed out of town, keeping to the right, and following the river closely till after crossing small iron bridge (2½ m.), when take second L. road, which follow direct to sign at L. (7½m.) which reads — "Lake George." Skirt shore of Lake from this point. Road generally good surface, with some hills. Good hotel at Lake. Here a good dinner can always be had — also repair kit, kept for convenience of visiting wheelmen by the Skowhegan Wheel Club.

SKOWHEGAN TO FAIRGRIEVES BAY (Hayden Lake) (6 m.). — Hotel Coburn up Madison street. Take first L. after crossing "Cold Brook" (¾ m.), then direct road and turn toward shore of lake soon after passing Madison Centre post-office. Good hotel, and repair kit as above. Roads very good; on direct route to Quebec, Canada.

SKOWHEGAN TO SMITHFIELD (9 m.). — Follow line of Skowhegan and Norridgewock Electric R. R. to South Norridgewock (5 m.) turn to L. at Sawyer House, then keep direct road. Some sand between Skowhegan and South Norridgewock; otherwise roads very good.

SKOWHEGAN TO BANGOR.

THROUGH ROUTE   **No. 34.**

Specific Directions.	Pass Through.	Road.	Distance.
Hazelton House, Water street R. At foot of Eddy Hill (bad) follow river R. to iron bridge, then second L., and direct to Canaan.	Canaan. *Pittsfield.* Newport. Ætna. Carmel. Hermon. ***Bangor.***	Fair; some hills. Excellent roads A1	9 Miles. 11 " 7 " 11 " 3 " 7 " 7 "
			55 Miles.

A fine run. The road is hard and gravelly. Hills of the long, gradual kind. A little sand just below the "Eddy" at Skowhegan, but free from it after 2 m. from that place. Said to be "best 50 m. in the State." Road from Pittsfield to Carmel very good. Many fine coasts all along the route.

Another way from Pittsfield to Carmel is by way of Detroit (4 m.), Plymouth (6 m.), South Etna (7 m.), Carmel (3 m,) One mile shorter, although former route considered the better.

At Newport is G. A. R. picnic ground, Camp Benson, 1½ miles from villlage. Good fishing on Sebasticook. Fine fishing at Hermon.

WATERVILLE TO BANGOR—Through Fairfield (2 m.), Clinton (6 m.), Burnham (5 m.), to Pittsfield (7 m.), and from there same as route above described.

HOTELS—CANAAN, Furber's Hotel, $. PITTSFIELD, Lancey House, $2.00. NEWPORT, Shaw House, $. BANGOR, Bangor House, $2.00., Windsor Hotel $1.50.

50

SKOWHEGAN TO MOOSEHEAD LAKE.

THROUGH ROUTE   No. 35.

Specific Directions.	Pass Through.	Road.	Distance.
Hazelton House, Water street north to "Dr. Man's" Plains ¼ mile. Turn R. across "Dr. Man's" Plains to Malborn Mills road, then take by-path side of road to Malborn Mills. Abbot to Greenville same as Route No. 32.	Malborn Mills. Cornville. Athens. Harmony. Cambridge. Parkman. Abbot (Lower). " (Upper). *Greenville.*	Generally very good,	3 miles. 5 " 4 " 8 " 5 " 10 " 1 " 23 "
			59 Miles.

At Moose Pond in Harmony, on direct road, is "Harmony Castle," owned by Boston and New York parties, who belong to the Megantic Fish and Game Club. They have an elegant building and fine grounds, and the place is worth a visit.

CANADIAN TOUR, SKOWHEGAN WHEEL CLUB. — 370 m. by wheel, 400 by steamer, 130 by rail. Through Kennebec valley to The Forks; then to Jackman's via Parlin's Pond and Owls Head. Over the boundary and up the Chaudiere valley, through St. George, St. Joseph, Beauce Junction, and St. Maries. Then more "St." towns, and 10 m. of macadam from St. Henri to Levis. Cross St. Lawrence to Quebec, and stop for side-runs to Montmorenci Falls (7 m.) and train to St. Anne (40 m.). Return to Quebec, then train to Roberval, and same to Chicoutimi, where take boat down Saguenay River to River du Loup. From thence south via Temiscouta district, Notre Dame du Lac, Edmonston, and follow St. John River to Grand Falls. Then 30 m. to Ft. Fairfield; next to Houlton, where train to Brownville, from thence wheel to Dexter, where ends the tour.

SKOWHEGAN TO MOOSE RIVER.

THROUGH ROUTE   No. 36.

SPECIFIC DIRECTIONS.	PASS THROUGH.	ROAD.	DISTANCE.
Hazelton House, Water St. L., Madison R. Take first L. after crossing small bridge, then direct to Madison Centre; then L. and direct to Patterson's Bridge. Then R. avoiding—	Madison Centre. Paterson's Bridge. Solon Ferry. Bingham. *The Forks.* Parlin Pond. *Moose River.*	Fair. One bad hill. Very good indeed.	5 Miles. 4 " 7 " 10 " 20 " 15 " 15 "
			76 Miles.

[SPECIFIC DIRECTIONS CONTINUED.]—North Anson, proceeding along river 5 miles, then turn to Solon Ferry, and on to Solon Village. Then cross small bridge to L. and follow direct road to Bingham. Turn L. at Forks for Moose River.

This run from Skowhegan to The Forks (and even to Canada) is about as good as macadam. The above route is an easy two days' ride.

The road from Patterson's Bridge to Salon Ferry is an elegant one, being alongside the river; only just before reaching the Ferry there is a hill which it is best to look out for.

BINGHAM TO THE FORKS is a remarkably fine road. Too much cannot be said in praise of it from a bicyclist's point of view.

Carrying Place Pond is located about half way between Bingham and The Forks, somewhat to the left of the road. This pond is noted for its red-spot trout, also as being the scene of Arnold's famous *faux pas* in his expedition to Quebec. It is related that Arnold proceeded up the Kennebec River to this point, then carried his boats overland to the above-named pond, and from thence to the Dead River, and so on to Quebec.

MOOSE RIVER TO MOOSEHEAD LAKE, take C. P. R. R. to Greenville Junction.

HOTELS—BINGHAM, Bingham Hotel, $2.00.

ROCKLAND TO BELFAST.

THROUGH ROUTE NO. 37.

SPECIFIC DIRECTIONS.	PASS THROUGH.	ROAD.	DISTANCE.
Thorndike House, Main street R. following telegraph poles N. W., almost straight road to Rockport. Follow telegraph poles Camden to Brown's Corner. Stage route. Then L. to Belfast.	*Rockport.* *Camden.* Lincolnville Beach. Saturday Cove, (Northport.) Brown's Corner, (Northport.) *Belfast.*	Most of the way very good.	6 Miles. 2 " 8 " 5 " 4 " 3 " 28 Miles.

The roads between Rockland and Rockport are fair to good, with two bad hills,—the "Clam Cove" hill rocky, and the other sandy.

Duck-Trap Hill, near Lincolnville, is not easy, but may be avoided by turning L. for 2 m. Spring-Brook Hill, north of Camden, is ¾ m. long, steep and dangerous.

At Saturday Cove take shore road (4 m.) through camp ground to Brown's Corner. Road somewhat hilly, but grand scenery; a fine view presented of Penobscot Bay and across to Islesboro.

ROCKLAND — Adjacent points of interest — Owl's Head and Crescent Beach (5½ m.); Tennant's Harbor (15 m.); Clark's Island (11 m.); Spruce Head (7½ m.); Bay Point (1½ m.); Oakland (4 m.).

It is a pleasant sail to take the steamer from Rockland to Bangor up the Penobscot River.

HOTELS — CAMDEN, Bay View House, $2.00; ROCKPORT, Carleton, $

SIDE-RUNS FROM BELFAST.

BELFAST TO ISLESBORO,—Start Crosby Inn down Franklin street to High, then R. to Commercial wharf, and take steamer (fare 50 cts.) to Rider's Cove (11 m.) Here leave hotel for a run L. to Lands End (7½ m.); or R. to Turtle's Head (9 m.)

ISLEBORO is one of the prettiest places that can be found on the coast, about 15 miles long, and well settled. The roads are good, and no better place can be selected for a week's outing, enjoying the wheeling, eating "clam roasts", shooting seals, etc. It is a sort of Maine Bermuda, so to speak.

HOTEL—Isleboro Inn, $. The island has excellent connections with Belfast, Bangor, Rockland, Bar Harbor and Castine by regular steamers after June 1st.

BELFAST TO MONROE VILLAGE via SWAN LAKE,—Start down Frrnklin street to High, R. to bridge, then straight on to Axe Factory, at which point turn L. to Y. of roads, where take L. leading direct to Swansville (7 m.) SWAN LAKE, 4 m. long by two wide, full of trout. There is also a steamer which will carry 50 people. On the east side of the lake a road runs to Clark's Corner and thence to Frankfort. This is one way to Bangor (36 m.) From SWANVILLE TO MONROE, (8 m.), take road west side of Lake, bearing always to R. via Lake Road. At Monroe is held the annual fair, which attracts the gentry of the country round. Roads generally good; all hills can be coasted.

BELFAST TO PITCHER'S POND (6 m.) After leaving city ascend a long hill, then L., then R., and direct to Pond. TILDEN'S POND (6 m.), on road to Searsmont, is a popular run passing near Belmont Corner. The route by this pond is sometimes taken to Searsmont Village. Good fishing at these ponds, and some cottage life.

BELFAST TO FORT POINT, (15 m.) Cross bridge and take shore road to Stockton via Searsport. At Searsport Cove ride out upon Sears Island (3 m.) for a side diversion. One-half mile from Stockton turn R. to Cape Jellison, and thence to Fort Point. Good road to Stockton, and fair to Cape; some hills. The Fort Point road is a pleasant one. Often wheelmen come from Bangor by boat to the Point, then wheel to Belfast. And from Belfast the boys often ride out during the camping season. It is a historic spot, having an old French fort said to have been built before the Revolutionary war. The early settlers traveled over this route to cross the river down to Castine to get their corn ground. There is also a lighthouse at the Point. It is considered the coolest place in Maine during the summer. The wind always blows, and it is necessary to keep up steam in the hotels.   HOTEL—Woodcliff, $.   Open after June 1st.

BELFAST TO CAMDEN.

Side Run	(VIA LINCOLNVILLE.)		No. 38.
Specific Directions.	Pass Through.	Road.	Distance.
From schoolhouse up Miller street to Lincoln Avenue. At Hall's Corner take L., as R. goes to Tilden's Pond and Searsmont. Then L., R., L., R. to Linville Centre, after which—	Hall's Corner. Dickey's Mills. Miller's Corner. Lincolnville Centre. *Camden.*	Fair. Some hills; do not coast. Some down grade.	5 Miles. 1 " 6 " 6 "
			18 Miles.

[SPECIFIC DIRECTIONS CONTINUED.]—Turn L. then R., and proceed by turnpike to Camden,

Another route to **LINCOLNVILLE.** After leaving Belfast proceed through Northport up a long hill, then turn L., then R. to Pitcher's Pond (6 m.), which is a popular run from Belfast. Proceed from pond S. W. to Miller's Corner, where take road above described. This route is not quite so good as the other.

From Lincolnville the turnpike is noted for its picturesque scenery, being built along the very base of Mount Megunticook, while the Lake of the same name is on the other side of the road not 20 feet away. It is a very popular drive for summer tourists. Hopkin's Milk Farm, a little way toward Camden, is the place to stop for refreshment. There is a pond on top of the mountain, but it is a hard climb to reach it. The place is fruitful of local legends, and worthy a visit from either Camden or Belfast. The return to Belfast may be made by way of the shore road, and the round trip will be 36 miles.

HOTEL—LINCOLNVILLE CENTRE, Maple House, $1.00.

BELFAST TO CASTINE.

THROUGH ROUTE. No. 39.

SPECIFIC DIRECTIONS.	PASS THROUGH.	ROAD.	DISTANCE.
High street north; turn R. at Phoenix House, Bridge street, cross bridge, follow water front to Searsport Harbor Cove, where turn L.; turn R. at schoolhouse, and again R. at Prospect P.O. Then —	Searsport. Prospect. Prospect Ferry. Bucksport. Orland. *Castine.*	Good. Rough. Fair.	6 Miles. 9 " 5 " 4 " 14½ " 39 Miles.

[SPECIFIC DIRECTIONS CONTINUED.] — Direct to River Road. Turn R. and L. to ferry, which cross to Bucksport. Thence to Orland and Castine, keeping river in view.

Castine is a town of historic note, possesses a deep harbor, and is a popular and growing resort for summer visitors.

ORLAND TO ELLSWORTH (17 m.) is the more direct through-route east.

BELFAST TO LIBERTY (16 m.). — Popular run through Belmont, Searsmont and South Montville. Road very fair. HOTEL — Sanford House.

BELFAST TO COTTAGE CITY INN (on Camden Turnpike) — 16¾ m.

BELFAST TO BANGOR.

THROUGH ROUTE   No. 40.

SPECIFIC DIRECTIONS.	PASS THROUGH.	ROAD.	DISTANCE.
Crosby Inn, Franklin street, by post office to High street, then L. to bridge; cross bridge and up "Bridge Hill", so called, turn R. on to Searsport road, then direct, following shore. Turn L. at—	Searsport. Stockton. Prospect. Frankfort. Winterport. Hampden. ***Bangor.***	Fair road. Good.	6 Miles. 4 " 4 " 4 " 3 " 8 " 5 " 34 Miles.

[SPECIFIC DIRECTIONS CONTINUED.]—Stockton, then L. and direct to Frankfort, and so on to Bangor, R. to Bangor House.

After leaving Stockton there is a sharp rise hard to climb, but the view is excellent from the top, taking in Penobscot Bay, the Islands, Camden Mountains, etc.; then down grade, and a fine run to Frankfort.

The Hampden drive is the finest near Bangor. Points of interest near Bangor—Pushaw Lake (9 m.) Phillips Lake (11 m.); hotels at both places. Also Hermon (8 m.) and Fields Ponds (7 m.)

Good hotels all along the route. At SEARSPORT, Searsport House, $1.50. STOCKTON SPRINGS, Stockton Springs Hotel, $1.50. WINTERPORT, Commercial House, $1.50. BANGOR, Bangor House, $2.00.

BANGOR TO MOOSEHEAD LAKE.

Through Route   (VIA KENDUSKEAG.)   **No 41.**

Specific Directions.	Pass Through.	Road.	Distance.
Bangor House, Union street to Hammond, then to Ohio street and direct to Kenduskeag. From Guilford same as Route No. 32.	*Kenduskeag.* East Corinth. West Charleston. Dover. Guilford. Abbot. Monson. Shirley. *Greenville.*	First class. Fair. Some hills.	11 Miles. 8 " 5 " 14 " 8 " 24 " 70 Miles.

Another route is via **DEXTER** (32 m.), through Exeter Mills (16 m.), and then proceed the same as Route No. 32. Road to Dexter fair, some hills, although considered the best road which enters that town. Or go east and north via Ripley, Cambridge, Parkman to Abbot, and from thence like Route No. 35.

The road from Bangor to Dover via Kenduskeag and East Corinth is pretty good and the country very picturesque. It is by far the best route to Moosehead Lake from this point.

Hotels—East Corinth, Parker House, $.   Dover, Blethen House, $2.00.   Dexter, Merchants Exchange, $2.00.

BANGOR TO BAR HARBOR.

THROUGH ROUTE (VIA ELLSWORTH) **No. 42.**

Specific Directions.	Pass Through.	Road.	Distance.
Bangor House, Main street R. to Exchange street. to L. to Washington street, over toll bridge to Brewer.	Brewer. Holden Centre. Dedham.	Good. Very hilly.	6 Miles. 6 "
ELLSWORTH—From post office, Main street, then R. to High street south over Trenton—	Ellsworth Falls. Ellsworth. ***Bar Harbor.***	Good deal of down grade.	10 " 4 " 21 "
			47 Miles.

[SPECIFIC DIRECTIONS CONTINUED.]—Road, Eden drive, Eden street, and so to Bar Harbor, passing through Salisbury and Hull's Coves, then take all turns to L. except by-roads. One bad hill—Beckworth's, a mile long; 10 m. to bridge; 11 m. bridge to Bar Harbor.

In Dedham township it is exceedingly mountainous, but those who have ascended the hills describe the view as very fine, and ample compensation for the labor of climbing. Three miles before reaching Ellsworth Falls, down grade and good coasts.

ANOTHER ROUTE is down the east side of river to Bucksport, (18 miles,) same as above to Brewer, then turn R. and follow river all the way on south and east side, then due east to Ellsworth through Orland (21 m.)

BUCKSPORT TO CASTINE (18 m.), via Orland, due south, which makes a Belfast connection with route to Bar Harbor.

From Castine to Sargentville (18 m.) via Penobscot; thence to Sedgwick (3 m.), Brooklin (4 m.), north to Blue Hill (12 m.), Surry (8 m.), Ellsworth (6 m.) Castine House, $1.50.

BAR HARBOR TO CHERRYFIELD 28 miles via Hancock and Franklin.

HOTELS—DEDHAM, Lake House, $, ELLSWORTH, Hancock House, $1.50.
BAR HARBOR, Hotel Brewer, $2.00, and Grand Central, $2.00. BUCKSPORT, Robinson House, $2.00.

MT. DESERT.

Mt. Desert is very irregular in outline, its shore being everywhere indented with bays, coves, creeks, and inlets. Its extreme length from north to south is 15½ miles, and its greatest width is 13 miles. It is separated from the mainland on the north and northeast and west by the Union River Bay and Blue Hill Bay. Its nearest approach to the mainland is at the narrows, where it is connected with the town of Trenton by a toll bridge ½ of a mile long. It has 13 distinct mountain peaks; Green Mountain is 1527 feet above sea level; Sargent's, 1344; Dry, 1268; Pemetic, 1262; Newport, 1060. These numerous mountain peaks constitute a vast watershed, which gives rise to many lakes and ponds. The best known of these is Eagle Lake, named by Church, the artist. It is about three miles from Bar Harbor, and is navigable by steamers; it also supplies Bar Harbor with water, and is 275 feet above the sea level. A striking feature of Mt. Desert is the rocky shore which extends nearly around it, rising at some points into bluffs, with perpendicular walls, against which the waves dash with ceaseless fury. The water is often thrown to a height of 15 feet, when it dashes against the sea wall at Southwest Harbor; and at Northeast Harbor a carriage road is built over one of these sea walls.

SIDE RUNS FROM BAR HARBOR.
THE OCEAN RIDE.

Take Main street south by the residence of Mr. G. W. Vanderbilt, turn L. at Y. and take shore road for about three miles to Schooners Head (where you can see the famous Spouting Horn, which blows after a storm), and Anemone Cave, then on to Great Head, and 3 miles farther to Otter Cliffs. At residence of Major Palmer turn R. and return by way of the Gorge. Distance in all about 13½ m. Road good, some hills, but easy to ride.

MAP Nº III.
FROM PENOBSCOT RIVER TO NEW BRUNSWICK.
Draughted by
F. L. Norris.

Scale of Miles

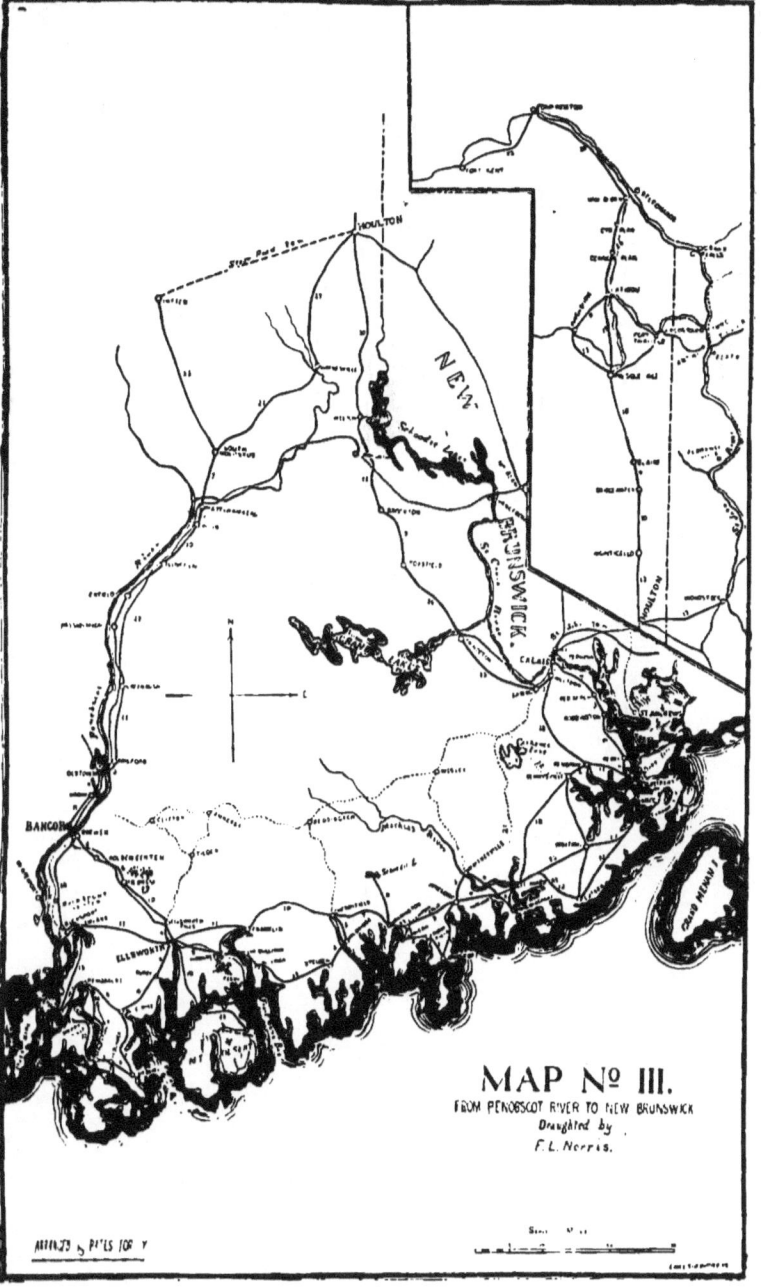

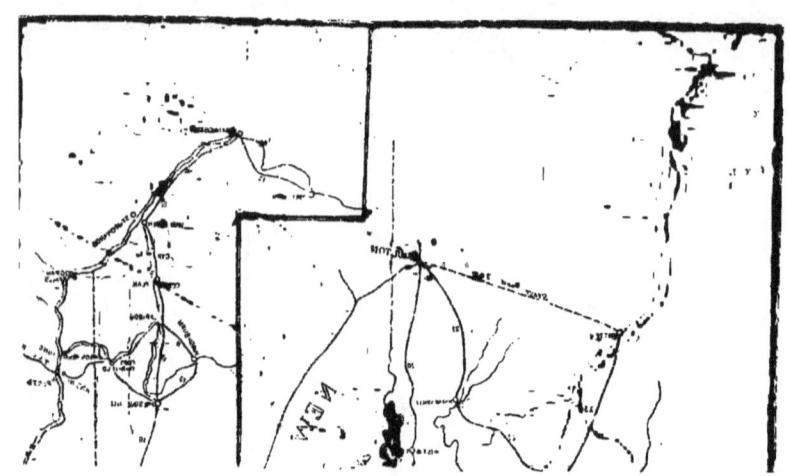

THE EAGLE LAKE RIDE.

Main street south to Mt. Desert street, which ends at Eagle Lake Road. Follow latter to foot of Green Mountain, past Kebo Club grounds, and on to the lake. Good fishing and boating or canoeing here. Steamer at Lake which runs in connection with Green Mountain railroad. Distance about 3 miles each way; road very hilly; return ride down grade. HOTEL — Lake House.

THE GREEN MOUNTAIN RIDE.

Main street to Mt. Desert street and Eagle Lake Road past Kebo Club grounds to guide board, which directs to Green Mountain carriage road. Distance about 2 miles from Bar Harbor, and about 2 miles farther to top of mountain. Another route is by way of Eagle Lake to foot of mountain (3 m.), and take cars to top for a coast down the carriage road. This is fine and exciting, being fully 3 miles long. Good hotel on top of mountain, — Summit House, — also fine view of the surrounding country.

THE 22 MILE RIDE.

So called because of being a round ride of 22 miles of interesting scenery. Main street south past Mr. G. W. Vanderbilt's residence, then turn R. at Y. of roads, then on through the Gorge. Turn R. at next Y. and direct to Seal Harbor, where may be seen a natural sea wall; then on to N. E. Harbor, and up Somes Sound between the upper and lower Hadlocks Ponds, through the Gorge between Brown and Sargent Mountains. Then turn R. at head of Sound into Somesville road, past Eagle Lake into Eagle Lake Road, past the foot of Green Mountain, on to Bar Harbor, down Mt. Desert street into Main street. Roads very fair and grade easy.

HOTELS at Seal Harbor, Northeast Harbor, and Eagle Lake.

Taking the Pennsylvania-Maryland-New Jersey-and-Delaware Road Book, which is comprised within one cover, in connection with this volume, the tourist will have directions practically covering the riding districts of the Eastern States, namely, Maine, Massachusetts, Vermont, Connecticut, Rhode Island, New York, New Jersey, Delaware, Maryland, District of Columbia, Pennsylvania, Virginia, Ohio, Illinois, and Missouri. L. A. W. members can buy this book for $1. Regular price $1.50.

ELLSWORTH TO MACHIAS.

THROUGH ROUTE   **No. 43.**

SPECIFIC DIRECTIONS.	PASS THROUGH.	ROAD.	DISTANCE.
Leave Ellsworth by Main street, continuing over Main street hill and on for 2 m., then bear L. into stage road and follow telegraph poles. Or proceed toward Hancock 6 m., then L. toward Franklin. 12 m. to Franklin by this way.	Franklin. Cherryfield. Harrington. Columbia Falls. Jonesboro. *Machias.*	Fair. Some hills, which favor rider going west.	11 Miles. 20 " 7 " 5½ " 8 " 9 "
			60¼ Miles.

Another route to **CHERRYFIELD** is through Hancock (9 m.), West Sullivan and Sullivan to Steuben (15 m.), thence to Millbridge (5 m.), and to Cherryfield (5 m.) This route follows the coast line more closely.

A few miles beyond Harrington turn R. toward Addison Point (5 m.), thence to Indian River (5 m.), and Jonesport (5 m.) From Jonesport to Machias (22 m.) via Jonesboro (12 m.) This also follows the shore somewhat. Addison Point to Jonesport is a good road down grade. Splendid trout brooks right on road.

JONESBORO to MACHIAS, another route, is to pass through Whitneyville; distance practically the same.

From Harrington go to Schoodic Lake for fine fishing (about 8 m.) Nice trout brooks near Jonesboro. A good opportunity for boating and picnics at Jonesport. Steamers connect twice a week for Portland.

HOTELS—Cherryfield House, $2.00.   JONESPORT, Bay View House, $2.00.   MACHIAS, Eastern Hotel, $1.50.

MACHIAS TO EASTPORT.

THROUGH ROUTE — **NO. 44.**

Specific Directions.	Pass Through.	Road.	Distance.
No particular directions; one principal thoroughfare.	East Machias. Whiting. Lubec. Ferry to Eastport.	A1. Very few hills; all rideable.	4 Miles. 12 " 12 "
			28 Miles.

Another way is via Cutler, following the coast line from East Machias. Distance same, good roads. Cathance Lake, 21 miles from Machias, best fishing ground in the State.

Customs of people dwelling on the road from Cutler to Lubec are rather quaint.

The spring tide rises at Eastport over 20 feet, which is the greatest height in the United States, and is almost twice that of any other locality.

"Every cyclist who takes advantage of an unprohibited sidewalk should first ride moderately, and then conduct himself with becoming deference towards all persons whose previous and better right to the ground is undisputable. When meeting a foot passenger he should exercise great caution in passing, and if the path be narrow, he should invariably dismount and take himself and his machine entirely out of the other's way; and when passing from the rear, the rider should take care to decently announce his coming from a respectful distance, and again dismount, unless the path be wide enough to allow him to pass mounted without inconvenience to the person walking."—*Conn. Road Book.*

MACHIAS TO CALAIS.

THROUGH ROUTE   **NO. 45.**

SPECIFIC DIRECTIONS.	PASS THROUGH.	ROAD.	DISTANCE.
From Eastern Hotel start east on Court street to strike road with telegraph poles. Machias to Pembroke follow telegraph poles. From Pembroke follow river west side 2½ m. north, then turn sharp R., cross bridge, go 2 m., then turn L. then R. at—	East Machias. Dennysville. Pembroke. Milltown. *Calais.*	Not an extra good road.	4 Miles. 18 " 6 " 18 " 2 "
			48 Miles.

[SPECIFIC DIRECTIONS CONTINUED.]—Guideboard, which says, "7 m. to Pembroke," then follow telegraph poles to Calais. This is more direct road than by way of Eastport. This route is 4 miles longer than the direct road from Machias to Calais, but it is more level. One can connect with the direct road 4 miles west of Pembroke.

A MORE DIRECT ROUTE.—Same as above to Dennysville, but just beyond turn L. at guide-board "21 m. to Calais," and follow telegraph poles.

Repair shop, Calais, Dr. F. H. Moore. Do not omit to run over (free bridges) to St. Stephen, N. B.; Y. M. C. A. Bicycle Club there.

From **PEMBROKE** southeast to Eastport, (11 m.) Pembroke has an extensive back country, full of game of all kinds. Dennysville to Cathance Lake, about (12 m.) northwest. Great fishing.

HOTELS — DENNYSVILLE, Riverside Inn, $2.00; CALAIS, Border City L. A. W., $1.50.

EASTPORT TO CALAIS.

THROUGH ROUTE   **No. 46.**

SPECIFIC DIRECTIONS.	PASS THROUGH.	ROAD.	DISTANCE.
From Quoddy Hotel follow Washington street straight out, and follow telephone poles. Toll bridge leaving Island. 5 cts. Keep R. at Y. just beyond bridge.	Perry. Robbinston. Red Beach. *Calais.*	Rolling. Most hills rideable. Fine run.	7 Miles. 9 " 3 " 9 "
			28 Miles.

 This road is the most beautiful in this section. It follows the shore of Passamaquoddy Bay and left bank of St. Croix River. Worst hills at Red Beach; dangerous to coast. Bad hill at South Robbinston, opposite the " Woodbine." A long coast between South Robbinston and Robbinston. From Perry visit village of Passamaquoddy Indians.
 At Red Beach are the largest red granite quarries in the world. Opposite is Douchets Island with lighthouse noted in history as being the site of the French settlement in 1605. Good roads in Calais, and road improvement is being agitated there quite strongly. Keep off sidewalks.
 Good mile-stones on this route from Robbinston to Calais (12 m.) "Calais Bicycle Club," Calais.
 Wheeling is very good in St. Stephen, N. B., the twin city across the bridge,. You can ride to St. John (70 m.), Moncton and Fredericton. It is a good sail from Eastport to Calais, touching at St. Andrews, N, B., and Robbinston, Me. At the former place there are considerable attractions presented in summer. A fine day's pleasure can be had at Eastport, deep sea fishing in the bay. Steamers leave daily for Lubec, Campobello and Grand Menan.
 HOTELS — Red Beach House, $2.00. ROBBINSTON, Brewer House, $2.00. SOUTH ROBBINSTON, Woodbine, $2.00. EASTPORT, The Quoddy, $1.50.

CALAIS TO HOULTON.

THROUGH ROUTE   **No. 47.**

SPECIFIC DIRECTIONS.	PASS THROUGH.	ROAD.	DISTANCE.
Border City Hotel. Start Main street north to N. Milltown street. Turn L. Keep this road through Milltown to Baring street, then turn L. following telegraph poles. Take first road at R. after leaving Milltown, diverging from telegraph poles here. Then simply keep main road straight on, which cannot be mistaken.	Milltown. Baring. Princeton. Topsfield. Brookton. (Jackson Brook.) Weston. ***Houlton.***	Good. Hilly. Generally good.	2 Miles. 3 " 15 " 16 " 9 " 15 " 30 "
			90 Miles.

HOULTON to WOODSTOCK, N. B., due east 12 miles. Very hilly.
Houlton is a very thriving place and the gateway to some fine wheeling north and into Aroostook county.

HOTELS—TOPSFIELD, Stewart's Hotel, $. Princeton House, $ BROOKTON, Baskahegan House, $. HOULTON, Snell House, $1.50.

HOULTON TO FORT KENT (126 m.) — via Caribou and Van Buren (see Routes Nos. 49 and 50). Makes a fine run through the northern portion of Aroostook County, sometimes called the "Garden of Maine."

BANGOR TO HOULTON.

Through Route — **No. 48.**

Specific Directions.	Pass Through.	Road.	Distance.
Bangor House, Main street, then direct road.	Orono.		8 miles.
	Oldtown.	Fair.	4 "
	Milford.		2 "
	Greenbush.		11 "
	Lincoln.		21 "
	Winn.	Some hills.	10 "
	Mattawamkeag.		2 "
	Junction of Patten Road (South Molunkus.)	Good.	7 "
	Haynesville.		21 "
	Houlton.		27 "
			113 Miles.

Patten, about 25 miles northwest of the Junction, is a good place to visit, being the terminus of the stage line from Mattawamkeag. There is a stage road from Patten to Houlton, about 30 miles as the crow flies.

Aroostook county contains 168 towns, plantations and townships. It is a vast domain. It abounds in water courses and lakes of great commercial utility, and picturesque to the eye. The wheeling roads are remarkably good, and were the county traversed by railroads, so that its resources could be developed, corresponding advantages would accrue in all directions. As it is the distances are wide, and there is much wild country; but the bicyclist will find the people hospitable, and the natural features of the region such as to make touring there very enjoyable.

HOTELS—Orono House, $. Winn Hotel, $. Mattawamkeag Hotel, $ South Molunkus Hotel, $. Patten Hotel, $. Houlton, Snell House, $1.50.

HOULTON TO PRESQUE ISLE.

THROUGH ROUTE   **No. 49.**

SPECIFIC DIRECTIONS.	PASS THROUGH.	ROAD.	DISTANCE.
HOTEL, Exchange, Court street, R. to Main, then direct road to Presque Isle. When within 3 to 3½ m. of Presque Isle turn L. at post office and store to Spragueville, a small town at the foot	Monticello. Bridgewater. Blaine. *Presque Isle.*	Good,	12 Miles. 8 " 6 " 16 "
			42 Miles.

[SPECIFIC DIRECTIONS CONTINUED.]—of the mountains, where the scenery is very fine.

Roads on this route comparatively good. Two bad hills—one in Monticello, and the other about 10 miles from Blaine, known as the "Winding Hill." At Blaine good trout fishing can be enjoyed at Jones's or Chandler's pond? Make a point to stop for dinner at the Blaine hotel.

If desired, take the Fort Fairfield road, which runs by the hotel, and proceed due north to Easton Centre (about 12 m.); there turn L. and proceed to Presque Isle through Sprague's Mills, a thriving village. Or continue straight from Blaine to Fort Fairfield, although the road is not so good as the one described in Route No. 50.

WOODSTOCK, N. B., on the St. John river, 12 or 13 miles east of Houlton, is reached via Richmond Corner, but the road is exceedingly hilly.

HOTELS—PRESQUE ISLE, West Side, $2.00. Blaine Hotel, $.

PRESQUE ISLE TO VAN BUREN.

Through Route   **No. 50.**

Specific Directions.	Pass Through.	Road.	Distance.
Main street, and when about a mile out of town, after crossing covered bridge, avoid turn to L., but keep straight on to Caribou.	*Caribou.* North Lyndon. Acadia. *Van Buren.*	Generally very good.	12 Miles. 5 5 12 "
			34 Miles.

With the exception of a few hills, and a particularly bad one within two miles of Caribou, the roads on this route are A1. The bad one referred to may be avoided by taking the new road recently completed, which will conduct the wheelman along the Aroostook River, where a good swim can be indulged in, or salmon fishing extraordinary. To gain this road make a turn R. about 20 rods beyond guideboard, which reads, "3 m. to Caribou."

Another route to Caribou is by way of Washburn (12 m.) as follows: Proceed north until across covered bridge, then L. and straight on, following right bank of Aroostook river. From Washburn across country northeast to Caribou (9 m.).

PRESQUE ISLE to FORT FAIRFIELD (10 m.)—Straight road northeast, making connection with the St. John river from Fort Fairfield to Andover, N. B. Or one can reach Andover from Caribou via Fort Fairfield. At Andover can connect with St John River route; see page 81.

This is a fine region for touring. The people are mostly French north of Caribou, but are very hospitable, and the hotel charges are reasonable.

Connection can be made with the St. Lawrence River region by way of Edmundston to Lake Temiscouata (31 m.), and from thence to Riviere de Loup, via St. Honore (50 m.), over excellent roads.

HOTELS—CARIBOU, Vaughan House, Burleigh House, $.

ROAD LAW.

Every thoroughfare which is, in the language of the English books, common to all the king's subjects, is a highway, whether it be a carriage-way, a horse-way, a foot-way, or a navigable river. (3 Kent Com., 432.)

So, too, the ways in public parks, being open to all the people, who are restricted only by the terms of their own enactment, which determine the uses for which the separate park-ways are dedicated and set apart, are, at least in the manner of their respective uses, public high-ways. (Commonwealth vs. Bowman, 3 Pa. St., 203; Commonwealth vs. Temple, 14 Gray, 74.)

Every member of the community has the right to travel upon the street or highway at all times, either on foot or by such means of conveyance as he may have or see fit to employ. (Coombs vs. Purrington, 42 Me., 332; Barker vs. Savage, 45 N.Y., 196.)

A street is made for the passage of persons and property, and the law cannot define what exclusive means of transportation and passage shall be used. . . . To say that a new mode of passage shall be banished from the streets, no matter how much the general good may require it, simply because streets were not so used in the days of Blackstone, would hardly comport with the advancement and enlightenment of the present age. (Moses vs. Pittsburgh, etc., R.R. Co., 21 Ill., 522.)

Persons making use of horses as a means of travel or traffic have no right upon the public highways superior to those who make use of the ways in other permissible modes. Improved methods of locomotion are admissible, and cannot be excluded from existing public roads, if not inconsistent with present methods. (Macomber vs. Nichols, 34 Mich., 212.)

The bicycle is a carriage, and wheelmen may go upon a public highway at all times possessed of the same rights, and liable only to the same restrictions to which the drivers of other carriages are subject.

The law favors courtesy, though it does not demand it, and in cases of trial at law a record of good manners goes far to win the favor of the court. (Extracts from "*The Law of Cycling,*" by ISAAC B. POTTER.)

Hotel or Restaurant	POINTS ON ROUTE (3)1	Total Distance from Start. Miles.	Distance Between Points.	Material of Road.	Grade of Road.	Condition of Road at its best.	Turns, Forks, General Instructions. T. L.=turn to left. L. F.=left fork. T. R.=turn to right. R. F.=right fork. T. F.=telegraph poles. X. R.=cross roads. See also "System of Abbreviation" facing Route (¶).
Grand, Clarendon	BOSTON (Copley Square)					good	T. R. Dartmouth St.; T. L. Commonwealth Ave.; T. R. Massachusetts Ave. (Chester Park), over Charles River, via Harvard Bridge, to Cambridgeport.
	CAMBRIDGEPORT	2.00	2.00			"	T. R. Windsor; cross electric car tracks direct to Webster Ave.; T. L. Webster Ave.
	UNION SQUARE, SOMERVILLE	3.50	1.50			"	T. R. Prospect St.; up small hill over R. R. tracks; T. R. Washington; T. L. Medford St. to Central Square to Winter Hill Station B. & M. R. R.
	WINTER HILL	4.25	.75			"	(At Central Sq. T. R. Cross St.; T. R. Mystic Ave.; T. L. Middlesex Ave. for Wellington and Malden.)
	MAGOUN SQUARE, MEDFORD LINE	5.00	.75			"	Medford St. direct, passing Mystic Park, to Medford.
Hawes	MEDFORD	6.50	1.50	macadam	level	"	Take Salem St., following horse-car tracks.
Evelyn	MALDEN	9.00	2.50	"	"	"	From City Square L. F. to church and pump; at pump T. R. Salem St. to Maplewood. (T. L. Main St., for Melrose, direct.)
	MAPLEWOOD	10.50	1.25	"	small hills	"	Salem St.; cross Newburyport Turnpike at ¼ m.; at ½ m. T. R. Beach St. for Revere Beach.
	FRANKLIN PARK	12.00	1.75	gravel	level	"	Salem St., direct; cross track at Franklin Park station.

Hotel or Restaurant.	POINTS ON ROUTE (3)2	Total Distance from Start. Miles.	Distance Between Points.	Material of Road.	Grade of Road.	Condition of Road at its best.	Turns, Forks, General Instructions. T. L.=turn to left. L. F.=left fork. T. R.=turn to right. R. F.=right fork. T. P.=telegraph point. X R.=cross roads. ☞ See also "System of Abbreviation" facing Route (1).
	CLIFTONDALE	12.75	.75	gravel	level	good	Salem St.; follow electric-car tracks.
	EAST SAUGUS	14.25	1.50	macadam	one hill	"	At fork at watering trough, L. F. Boston Street over Tower Hill; at horse-car station R. F., and at Commons St. T. L. for Common.
Revere H.	LYNN	16.50	2.25	"	level	good	Common St., T. L. at City Hall and follow Essex St. direct.
	UPPER SWAMPSCOTT	18.25	1.75	"	rolling	"	Continue on Essex and Lafayette Sts.; cross bridge in Salem and take Central St. over pavement; T. R. to Essex House.
Essex H.	SALEM	22.50	4.25	"	level	"	From Essex House pass through stable-yard; T. R. Church and Drown Sts. to Washington Square; T. L. to Winter St.; T. R. Bridge St. to Beverly.
Trafton	BEVERLY	24.00	1.50	gravel	"	"	At end of bridge T. R. and take second L. Rantoul St. and follow horse-car tracks.
	WENHAM	29.00	5.00	"	rolling	first-class	After passing station follow T. P. through Hamilton. Camp-Meeting at Asbury Grove, during summer.
Agawam	IPSWICH	35.75	6.75	"	small hills	"	Main St. T. R., then T. L., direct.
Eagle H.	ROWLEY	39.50	3.75	"	"	"	Through Rowley woods to Parker River. Good well at R. R. crossing.
	NEWBURY	44.25	4.75	oyster shell and gravel	level	"	Down Gravel Hill; fine coast; High St.; T. R. State St. to hotel.

Hotel or Restaurant.	POINTS ON ROUTE (3)3	Total Distance from Start. Miles.	Distance Between Points.	Material of Road.	Grade of Road.	Condition of Road at its best.	Turns, Forks, General Instruction. T. L.=turn to left. L. F.=left fork. T. R.=turn to right. R. F.=right fork. T. P.=telegraph poles. X. R.=cross roads. ☞ See also "System of Abbreviation" facing Route (1).
Wolf Tavern	NEWBURYPORT	48.25	4.00	gravel	level	good	Follow electric car tracks to the west to Chain Bridge; this is the best route for T. L. from hotel, Harris St. into Washington; right Winter St., over Merrimac River Bridge; road to Salisbury. Roads poor. Fair side-path riding to Seabrooks).
	CHAIN BRIDGE	50.75	2.50	"	hilly	"	Take 2d T. R.; do not go into the centre of Amesbury; about ¼ mile from Chain Bridge T. R.; notice Portsmouth sign-board; pass Rocky Hill Church, built 1796.
American	AMESBURY	51.75	1.00	"	level	"	Continue as above, following T. P.; take L. of Rocky Hill Church.
	SEABROOK	55.75	4.00	sandy	"	fair	Follow T. P.
Union H.	HAMPTON	59.50	3.75	gravel	"	good	Two roads — the Lafayette road, inland, is direct; T. R. for shore route. If not in haste, take shore route for beautiful scenery to Newcastle; this road passes Rye Beach, Little Bore's Head, and other points of interest.
Rockingham.	PORTSMOUTH	70.50	11.00				

Hotel or Restaurant.	POINTS ON ROUTE (4)						
	BOSTON	0.00		Via	Route	3.	Via Route (3); see also Routes (31) (32) (33).
Revere	LYNN	10.50	4.00	gravel	level	good	Market St.; T. L. Broad St.; R. F. Beach St.; after crossing isthmus take first R., which is hilly, leads to Relay House; second R. level, then first L. leads through town; fine view of ocean.
Relay H.	NAHANT	20.50					

Hotel or Restaurant	POINTS ON ROUTE (2)	Total Distance from Start. Miles.	Distance Between Points.	Material of Road.	Grade of Road.	Condition of Road at its best.	Turns, Forks, General Instructions. T. L.=turn to left.　　L. F.=left fork. T. R.=turn to right.　　R. F.=right fork. T. P.=telegraph pole.　　X. R.=cross roads. ☞ See also "System of Abbreviation" facing Route (1).
Grand, Clarendon	BOSTON (Copley Square)	0.00					Via Route (1).
			34.50	Via	Route	(1)	
Northboro	NORTHBORO	34.50					Main St. R. F. at fountain; R. F.; across bridge, at 1¼ m., R. F. Take main road beyond saw-mill; good coasting. Watch sign boards.
			2.50	gravel	level	good	
	SOUTH BERLIN	37.00					Direct, or T. L. Pass in rear of railroad station. Blacksmith shop on edge of Berlin.
			2.50	"	rolling	"	
	BERLIN	39.00					T. R. beyond blacksmith shop ; direct to L. for Clinton. Keep to L. of M. C. R. R.
			2.00	"	level	"	
	WEST BERLIN	40.50					T. R. under railroad bridge ; pass schoolhouse and bear L. ; R. F. down hill ; T. R. across bridge ; L. F. at watering trough. Next R. is High St. to Clinton.
			1.50	"	small hills	"	
Clinton H.	CLINTON	42.00					Take High St. across railroad, direct to large barn on corner ; T. R.; pass saw-mill and under W. N. R. R. Up grade to South Lancaster.
			2.50	"	level	"	
	SOUTH LANCASTER	44.00					Main St., left of watering trough to bridge, L. F. after crossing bridge. Up grade to Lancaster.
			1.00	"	"	"	
	LANCASTER	46.50					Main St., front of church, to bend in street, to L.; bear to left, with Main St. to hotel ; at bend (R. F. for Shirley, Ayer, and Nashua, N. H.)
			2.50	"	rolling	"	
	NORTH LANCASTER	47.50					Over Ballard's Hill ; pass Lancaster Poor Farm. Surface good, but from saw-mill on further side, road sandy and poor. Side path riding about 4 miles.
			1.00	gravel and sand	hilly	"	
Leominster	LEOMINSTER	52.00					Main road—side of O. C. R. R. all the way. Usually good, but in dry weather gets cut up.
			4.50	"	level	poor	
Fitchburg	FITCHBURG	57.00					
			5.00			fair	

Hotel or Restaurant.	POINTS ON ROUTE (1)1	Total Distance from Start, Miles.	Distance Between Points.	Material of Road.	Grade of Road.	Condition of Road at its best.	Turns, Forks, General Instructions. T. L.=turn to left, L. F.=left fork, T. R.=turn to right, R. F.=right fork, T. P.=telegraph poles, X. R.=cross roads. See also "System of Abbreviation" facing route (1).
Grand, Clarendon	BOSTON (Copley Square)	0.00		macadam	level	good	T. R. Dartmouth St. ; T. L. Commonwealth Ave. into Beacon St. Boulevard, and follow electric car tracks to Chestnut Hill Reservoir.
	CHESTNUT HILL RESERVOIR	5.25	5.25	"	hilly	"	"Wheelmen's Rendezvous." Good well at back of stone cottage. After leaving "Rendezvous" take first R. Beacon St, up long hill. Then two excellent coasts to Newton Centre.
	NEWTON CENTRE	6.50	1.25	hard gravel	small hills	"	Follow Beacon St. direct.
	GREAT SIGN BOARDS	9.50	3.00	"	level	"	Follow Washington St.
	NEWTON LOWER FALLS	10.25	.75	"	hilly	"	Cross R. R. and up long hill. Coast with caution coming toward Newton Lower Falls.
	WELLESLEY HILLS	11.75	1.50	"	level	"	At watering-trough in front of hotel. L. F.
Hagar H.	WELLESLEY	13.00	1.25	"	"	"	R. F. Central St. (For South Natick, L. F. [2.15 m.] Bailey's Hotel.)
Wilson	NATICK	16.00	3.00	gravel	"	"	Direct road. Pass Lake Cochituate.
Old Colony H.	SOUTH FRAMINGHAM	19.75	3.75	gravel and clay	"	"	Concord St. cross R. R. T. L. Union Ave.

Hotel or Restaurant.	POINTS ON ROUTE (1)2	Total Distance from Start. Miles.	Distance Between Points.	Material of Road.	Grade of Road.	Condition of Road at its best.	Turns, Forks, General Instructions. T. L.=turn to left. L. F.=left fork. T. R.=turn to right. R. F.=right fork. T. P.=telegraph poles. X. R.=cross roads. See also "System of Abbreviation" facing route (1).
Central H.	FRAMINGHAM	22.00					Pass R. R. station, take direct road by southwest side of Sudbury River Basin ; ½ mile beyond leave T. F. R. F. under R. R. bridge, T. L., then R. F., thus avoiding Fayville.
	SOUTHBORO	28.50	2.25	gravel	rolling	good	
Northboro Hotel	NORTHBORO	34.50	6.50	"	"	"	From Main Street to Burnett's, then R. F. to foot of next hill, then R. F. and follow direct road.
	SHREWSBURY	39.50	5.00	"	hilly	"	Main St. L. F. at street fountain. Direct road.
	LAKE QUINSIGAMOND	42.50	5.00	gravel and sand	"	fair	Beyond church L. F. in centre of town, taking new road. Descend long hill with care. Nearly all up and down grade.
Lincoln H. Bay State	WORCESTER	44.50	3.00	gravel and macadam	"	good	Old College Regatta Course to north of Causeway a good stiff climb of ½ of a mile to Insane Asylum. Road cut up from heavy teaming.
			2.00				From Union Depot take Mechanic and Church Streets to City Hall.
	POINTS ON ROUTE (1)A						
Grand, Clarendon	BOSTON	0.00			Route	(2)	Via Route (2).
Clinton H.	CLINTON	43.00		gravel	hilly	good	Pass R. R. station and at sign board R. F. Red Stone Hill is a stiff climb. Descend carefully to Sterling.
	STERLING	48.50	5.50	gravel and sand	"	fair	Go slow on hills unless you can see bottom. Last two miles mostly up hill. Fair side path riding.
	EAST PRINCETON	53.25	4.75	gravel, rough, stony	"	"	One-half mile from East Princeton T. L. About half distance is fair riding, and the rest up hill to the hotel.
Summit H.	MT. WACHUSETT	55.50	2.25	*		"	A fine view can be had from top of the mountain, and it will well repay you for climbing it. Summit house top of mountain. Mt. House base of mountain.

Hotel or Restaurant.	POINTS ON ROUTE (59)1	Total Distance from Start. Miles.	Distance Between Points.	Material of Road.	Grade of Road.	Condition of Road at its best.	Turns, Forks, General Instructions. T. L. =turn to left. f. F.=left fork. T. R.=turn to right. R. F.=right fork. T. P.=telegraph poles. X R.=cross roads. ☞See also "System of Abbreviation" facing Route (1).
Fitchburg	FITCHBURG	0.00					
	WEST FITCHBURG	1.50	1.50	macadam and gravel	level	fair	T. L. River St. and pass under R. R. bridge.
	WESTMINSTER	7.00	5.50	clay	hilly	"	T. R. at Waiti's corner and continue direct.
South Gardner	SOUTH GARDNER	10.75	3.75	loam	rolling	good	T. L. above Nichols Bros.' chair shop. Direct road.
Bay State H.	EAST TEMPLETON	14.25	3.50	sand	small hills	fair	Direct road.
Templeton	TEMPLETON CENTRE	15.75	1.50	sandy loam	hilly	poor	Follow T. P. One very hard hill. Good scenery.
	BROOK'S VILLAGE	17.75	2.00	"	"	fair	Take road between two brick buildings. T. L. and continue direct.
Commercial	ATHOL	24.25	6.50	loam	"	"	Direct road. From top of hill in B. V. bear a little to the R. At four corners keep straight road.
	ORANGE	31.25	7.50	sand	very hilly	good	Direct.
	MILLER'S FALLS	41.55	10.30	"	"	"	Direct, via West Orange; Wendell, 5½, and Erving, 5.70.
Farrin H.	TURNER'S FALLS	46.55	5.00	sand and loam	"	"	Direct.
Mansion H.	GREENFIELD	50.30	3.75	sand	hilly	fair	Direct. Cross Suspension Bridge and follow T. P.

SHELBURNE	55.30	3.50	"	"	"	T. R. up hill and follow T. P. direct.
SHELBURNE FALLS	58.80	4.50	"	"	bad	Cross river and follow T. P. Riders had better take cars here for North Adams.
EAST CHARLEMONT	63.30	4.50	sand	"	"	Direct.
CHARLEMONT	67.80	4.50	"	"	"	Direct; hard walking, but good scenery.
ZOAR	72.30	4.30	railroad track	rolling	fair	On R. R. track, frequent dismounts, but better than the road.
HOOSAC TUNNEL STATION	76.60	10.00	sand and rocks	mountain	bad	Up mountain to summit; hard climbing, with only occasional riding.
NORTH ADAMS	86.60	7.00	loam	rolling	good	Take Main St. over Furnace Hill.
WILLIAMSTOWN	93.60	7.50	loam and gravel	hilly	"	From Mansion House T. R., then direct and cross R. R., then T. L. and go through Pownal.
NORTH POWNAL, Vt.	101.10	4.70	"	"	"	Direct.
NORTH PETERSBURGH, N. Y.	105.80	23.50	stone road	"	"	T. R. and at 1½ m. at Stone Church, T. L. on to "Old Stone Road," which goes direct to Troy, via Pittstown, Raymerstown, and other small places.
TROY	129.30	7.20	macadam & pavement	level	fair	Cross Congress St. bridge to West Troy, and then follow horse-car tracks.
ALBANY	136.50					

Hotel or Restaurant.	POINTS ON ROUTE (22)1	Total Distance from Start. Miles.	Distance Between Points.	Material of Road.	Grade of Road.	Condition of Road at its best.	Turns, Forks, General Instructions. T. L.=turn to left. L. F.=left fork. T. R.=turn to right. R. F.=right fork. T. P.=telegraph poles. X. R.=cross roads. See also "System of Abbreviation" facing Route(1).
Grand, Clarendon	BOSTON (Copley Square)	0.00				good	Huntington Ave.; T. L. Parker St.; T. L. Tremont St.; T. R. New Heath St.; T. L. Parker St.; T. R. Centre St. to J. P.
			3.75				
	JAMAICA PLAIN	3.75				"	Take South St. L. of Monument; T. L. at watering-trough.
			2.10				
	FOREST HILL STATION	5.85					Cross R. R. track and T. R. Walkhill St.; R. F. Hyde Park Ave.
			1.50				
	CLARENDON HILLS	7.35					Follow Hyde Park Ave. and its continuation, Central Park Ave.; T. R. River St.
			2.00				
	HYDE PARK	9.35					Cross square and take Centre St., River St.; at Milton St., T. R.
			2.00				
	EAST DEDHAM	11.35					T. L. High St.
			1.00				
Norfolk House	DEDHAM (Memorial Hall)	12.35					Washington St. direct.
			4.10				
	NORWOOD (Public Library)	16.45				"	R. F. after passing Norwood Village.
			4.40				
	WALPOLE (Town Hall)	20.85				fair to good	T. L. at Common; ¼ m., T. R., and continue to turn-pike; T. R. to So. Walpole. In So. W., T. L. direct through No. Foxboro.
			6.60				
Cocasset House	FOXBORO CENTRE	27.45				"	Bear to R. of Common, and T. R. South St. direct at first cross-road (2.55 m.), continue straight to fork; L. F. to turn of road; bear R., cross Wading River and continue to fork beyond reservoir; L. F. to end; T. R. Pleasant St. to Park St.; T. R. across R. R. to fountain.
			9.75				
Park Hotel	ATTLEBORO	37.20				"	T. L. So. Main St. to car track and follow
			2.30				
	DODGEVILLE (Bridge)	39.50					

" Hotel or Restaurant.	POINTS ON ROUTE (22)2	Total Distance from Start, Miles.	Distance between Points.	Material of Road.	Grade of Road.	Condition of Road at its best.	Turns, Forks, General Instructions. T. L.=turn to left. L. F.=left fork. T. R.=turn to right. R. F.=right fork. T. P.=telegraph poles. X. R.=cross roads. ☛ See also "System of Abbreviation" facing route (Y).
	DODGEVILLE. (Bridge)	39.50	1.40			fair to good	Follow car track.
	HEBRONVILLE (Bridge)	40.90	1.75			fair	Follow car track. Cross Lebanon Bridge.
	LEBANON MILLS	42.65	2.30			good	Continue straight Central Ave. and follow car track to first 6 corners; L. F. with car track; Cottage St. to junction of car tracks.
	PAWTUCKET, R. I. (Summit Street)	44.95	5.30			"	T. L. Summit St.; first R. Main St., bearing L. at forks; first L. School St., bearing R. at forks to first cross street; T. R. Division St., across river; T. L. Pleasant St., becoming Seven Point Road at Providence line; first L. beyond the cemetery; Blackstone Boulevard to end; continue Butler Ave., following car track, and T. R. Angell St., continue to Asylum wall; third L. Cooke St.; fourth R. Benevolent St. to end; R. Benefit St.; second L. College St., and down hill into Market Sq.
	PROVIDENCE, R. I.	59.25				"	

By courtesy of the Road-book Committee of the Massachusetts Division we are permitted to reprint the foregoing tabulated pages from their Road-book. This enables us to complete a continuous description of roads from Boston to the Provinces, as well as present a few routes radiating from "The Hub" — for the benefit of visitors from Maine.

BOSTON RIDING DISTRICT : Draw a line around and including the following towns, — Newburyport, West Newbury, Newbury, Rowley, Topsfield, Peabody, Lynnfield, Stoneham, Winchester, Waltham, parts of Weston and Wayland, Framingham, Natick, Dover, Medfield, Walpole, Sharon, Easton, Bridgewater, East Bridgewater, Abington, Hingham and Cohasset. The entire area included between this line and the ocean affords continuous first-class riding, with few exceptions. The immediate vicinity of Boston has its own reputation for excellent roads, and no comment is necessary.

The bicycle is held by the common law decisions of both countries to be a carriage. So decided in this country by the Government authorities at Washington, under advice of the law department, in the case of Chandler (1887); also by N. H. Supreme Court in Ladd v. Allen (1881), and so regarded by Common Councils of Boston, Brooklyn and other cities, under advice of eminent legal counsel in ordinances relating to use of streets. The rider of the bicycle is the driver of a carriage, and as such entitled to the rights and privileges specified in Chapter lxx of the Revised Statutes of Maine, being the law of the road in this State.

A NEW BRUNSWICK RUN.

EDMUNDSTON to ST. JOHN. — From Edmundston (28 m. from Van Buren, N. W.), take the right-hand road after crossing the bridge from Hotel Hebert, then pass through St. Basile (5 m.), and ride as far as Green River, 8 m. below Edmundston. Three miles below Green River is Prince Terrio's, where you can stop for dinner. You then pass on to St. Leonards, and from there to Grand Falls, which is 40 miles from Edmundston, over a clayish road. At the Falls you stop at Grand Falls Hotel; from here proceed to Andover (24 m.) over a good road, and stop at the Newcomb House. This is just below the mouth of the famous Tobique River, where there is some very fine salmon and trout fishing — about two hours drive to the fishing ground. There are two roads from Andover to Fort Fairfield, Me., one about 7 miles long, and the other about 12 miles. From Andover follow the telegraph poles to Florenceville (27 m.), over fair roads, and most of the few hills there are favor the bicyclist riding down river from the Falls. The hotel at Florenceville is situated on the opposite side of the St. John River, and on top of a high hill. To get to it cross the bridge, and climb the hill. It is known as Tracy's Hotel.

There are three roads leading from Florenceville to Woodstock; one follows the St. John River, another takes the right bank for 10 m., then turns at right angles from the river and proceeds about 6 m., then turns L., leading into Upper Woodstock, a distance of 3 m. more. Each of these roads is about 16 m. long. From Florenceville the third road runs at a direct right angle from the river for 4 m. over a hilly road to Centreville, a very lively village. Thence almost direct to Upper Woodstock. Distance from Florenceville to Woodstock this way is about 23 m. Upper Woodstock is about two miles from Woodstock proper. The hotels at Woodstock are Willows, Exchange and Victoria.

NOTE. — Another recommendation is to follow the right bank of the river to Andover, then cross to Woodstock. Then take the right bank to Fredericton, and train to St. John. There is also a place above Woodstock where a crossing may be made to the right bank, and from there the wheeling is better.

From Woodstock to Fredericton is about 64 m. over a good road, through beautiful scenery. At Eel River, 13 m. from Woodstock, is a village and a hotel. The half-way house is about 34 m. from Woodstock, and is a very good place to put up for a night, or stop for a day or two.

From Fredericton to St. John there are two roads, one about 68 m. long, while the other is about 70 m. The old "Nerepis" road is 68 m., and fair going, 12 m. of which is through woods without a dwelling of any kind, but is very good wheeling, being the old stage road; 35 m. from Fredericton is the half-way house. The other road goes to Oromocto (11 m.). From Oromocto turn L. and ride to Gagetown (12 m.), passing through Upper Gagetown. Gagetown is a village of considerable size, and a great resort for city people in summer time. The distance from Gagetown to St. John is equal to a forty mile ride, or the tourist can take the steamer which runs down the river every day. The best hotels in St. John are the Royal, Victoria, and Dufferin.

A LITTLE TALK ABOUT ROADS.

THE wheelman as he tours through Maine will, without doubt, be impressed with the fact that there might be better roads than those over which he is travelling. He will find sandy roads, rocky roads, clay roads (that after a rain resemble nothing so much as glue), and roads that select all the hills, and climb over them with a persistency worthy of a better cause. He will notice that the grading is extremely erratic — sharp pitches that call for skilful management in their descent, or weariness of flesh if the way is toward the summit.

Once in a while, as compensation for the above evils, he will come upon a bit of good riding, a smooth surface, an easy grade beneath overhanging trees, through whose branches the rays of the sun are sifted pleasantly, and perhaps a rushing river to keep him cheerful company. Then he will wonder why it cannot always be thus, and what the reason is for our poor highways.

The explanation is not difficult to make. To begin with, Maine is not a wealthy State, and good roads cost money. Much of the territory is but sparsely settled, and the tax per capita *at the start* would be more than the average inhabitant thinks necessary, just so long as he can get from place to place, even at the expense of much horseflesh, harness and vehicles, to say nothing of time and temper.

Secondly, our system of allowing the citizen to work out his taxes on the road is about as bad a one as could be devised. With little or no knowledge of road-building, a semi-holiday affair is made of the matter, and he who can spend the most time in doing the least work is the best fellow. The said "work" generally consists of shovelling the dirt from the roadside into the middle of the street, thereby rendering it almost impassable for several weeks, until worn down by the teams which often crawl along one side or the other, leaving a ridge in the centre. The "making" of the road is generally in the hands of a selectman, whose knowledge of the milk business, or ability to run a country store, is supposed to give him peculiar fitness for the position.

In the early days it is said that many of the Maine roads were laid out by the surveyors taking "sights" from the top of one hill to another. This accounts for many of the abandoned roads that are to be met leading over some steep inclines, while the new highway winds around the foot of the hill — a striking proof that "the longest way round is the shortest way home."

The "working out" system, and the running of roads from hilltop to hilltop, had excuse for being when the country was new, men were scarce, and the lowlands were covered with a dense forest; but circumstances have changed, and the time has come when we should pause and consider how much better and *cheaper* it would be for all, if our wretched roads were transformed into smooth, well-graded and well-drained highways. It has been done in other countries, and it can be done here.

Napoleon early in his career saw the necessity of roads over which he could draw his cannon in all weathers to all points of the frontier of France. He summoned his most skilful engineers, and directed them to lay out a system of *national* roads radiating from Paris to all parts of his empire, good for all time and seasons. To say with him was to do, and now France is traversed by a network of roads that would cause the heart of a Maine cyclist to bound for joy. They are broad as a river, smooth as a floor, often shaded by trees, and so finely graded that I have often seen wheelmen attempt to coast on an up-grade under the impression that they were going down hill. The loads that are hauled on these roads are perfectly astonishing. Enormous loads of hay that tower to the tops of the trees come slowly along, making the powerful Norman draught horses seem like ponies by comparison with the load they are drawing. A covered van, big enough to contain all the furniture of a good-sized household, is seen transporting the goods of some Frenchman with the whole family on top. How easily it rolls along. In this country it would take ten horses to move it, and the road would look like a ploughed field after its passage; here three horses are enough, and not a dent is made in the road. Then a company of artillery, the heavy canonry thundering along with a jingling accompaniment of sabres and spurs. I remember seeing a small house on wheels, drawn by one horse, the proprietor sitting in a chair on the front porch, holding the reins with one hand, and supporting a long pipe with the other. Inside culinary operations were in progress, as evidenced by smoke issuing from the chimney-pipe.

Other European countries have followed the example of France, and now England, Italy, Germany, Switzerland, Norway and Sweden can boast of roads but little inferior to those we have described. The first cost of these roads is, of course, quite heavy, but no jobbery is permitted; and once made they are kept with the greatest care, and with a less annual expenditure than for our apologies for the same thing. Road material is always ready, and worn places quickly repaired. Often one may see the local roadman carefully trimming away the encroaching turf with a guiding-line, or sweeping any foreign matter into little piles to be carted away; and all this, far out in the country, miles from any habitation.

Now, this is what we want, if it is a possible thing; and there is no reason why it should not be possible. Our roads should be built by men skilled in the business, who have studied engineering, the various kinds of soil, and the best way of treating them. They should be familiar with the various methods employed by the leading road-makers of the world, — MacAdam, Telford, and others, and should be held responsible for all roads built under their supervision.

These men would command a high price, and would be worth it. Then, when a road is to be built or repaired, construct as much as possible in the best manner, and let the rest go until that can be treated in the same way. Thus we should eventually have good roads, and the saving in harnesses, wagons, time and temper would be beyond calculation. Each year the number of summer visitors to our State increases; for our beautiful lakes, mountains and sea-coast possess attractions unequalled by other regions, and a large amount of money is left with us each year by the seekers for health and pleasure. Maine is fast becoming the great summer resort of the inhabitants of the eastern States, and it behooves us to do all in our power to attract and retain them.

For this reason, if nothing more, it would be appropriate and wise for the State to undertake a system of State highways. How much this would add to our prosperity can be easily seen by one who has visited Switzerland. Every cent spent upon their wonderful roads has returned to them a hundred-fold, and the same result would obtain here without the shadow of a doubt.

Let us keep these things in mind, and work to that end.

F. A. ELWELL.

THE CAMPAIGN OF ENLIGHTENMENT.

LET him who consults this book, which shows the highways and byways of Maine, pause and consider — not alone the bicyclist who seeks easy paths, but him who drives for enjoyment, him who carries the products of the farm to market — let them all pause and understand that the League of American Wheelmen is the leader in the movement to add pleasure to the pleasure-seeker, profit to the bread-winner, and prosperity to the State in which they live.

Why is that piece of road near your town always muddy or dusty, and never good, in spite of the days of labor and scores of dollars that every year during your lifetime have been spent upon it? Because it never was properly repaired. Why not? Because ignorance and false economy have ruled the town meeting; because the old system of working out taxes has been adhered to, and scientific methods have been ignored. How much pleasanter — how much more profitable, if it were otherwise! And it might be.

It is one of the functions of the League of American Wheelmen to educate the people in this direction; to show them how properly to build and maintain a road; to demonstrate that the good highway is not simply better than the poor one — but cheaper. Therefore ponder! Is not the campaign of enlightenment worthy of support? Consider if it is not for your individual interests so to have the matter presented that the Legislature shall take action, and State aid to the work be secured.

Opposition means unenlightenment, and but serves to bring out in stronger light that the most important factor in the development of the State of Maine, the surest, quickest, cheapest, and — considering geographical position — almost the only path to State advancement, is by methodical, scientific construction of the great highways.

JAMES E. MARRETT, *Chief Consul, Maine Division L. A. W.*

BICYCLE REPAIRERS.

BANGOR . . . . C. H. Barstow.	KENNEBUNK . . . . . W. H. Littlefield.
BELFAST . . . . . . George T. Read.	LEWISTON . . . . Hanscome & Lane.
BETHEL . . . . F. M. Allen.	NORWAY . . . . Swett & Sessions.
BIDDEFORD . . . . . R. A. Fairfield.	OLDTOWN . . . . C. A. Dillingham.
BIDDEFORD . . . . . . W. T. S. Morrison.	PITTSFIELD . . . . . . T. G. Lancy.
CALAIS . . . . F. H. Moore.	PORTLAND . . . . . . Haggett Bros.
CAMDEN . . . . G. A. Sobin.	ROCKLAND . . . . . . W. M. Purrington.
FAIRFIELD . . . . . J. P. Lawry.	SANFORD . . . . G. R. Bodwell.
HOULTON . . . . . . Harry Lane.	

CHARGES FOR TRANSPORTATION.

Grand Trunk R. R.	One wheel with passenger	No charge.
Portland & Rochester R. R.	One wheel with passenger	No charge.
Portland Steam Packet Co.	One wheel with passenger	No charge.
Maine Steamship Co.	One wheel with passenger	50 cents.
International S. S. Co.	One wheel with passenger	$1.00
Boston & Maine R. R.	One wheel with passenger	25 cents.
Maine Central R. R.	One wheel with passenger	25 cents.

INDEX.

REMARK — Wheelmen wishing to make up through routes covering greater distances, can combine the numbers; or reverse them, if desiring to travel in an opposite direction.

	PAGE
Acton Corner	14
A little Talk about Roads — F. A. Elwell	82–85
Alfred to Biddeford	14
Andover to Upton	41
Aroostook County	67
Around Lake Auburn	36
Auburn to Lake Auburn	32
" " Norway	38
Augusta to Belfast	43
" " Farmington	44
" " Rockland	45
" " Skowhegan (via Waterville)	44
" " Togus	43
" " Waterville (via Sidney)	44
" and Winslow to China Pond	44
" to Winthrop	43
Bath to Birch Point	12
" " Small Pt., Ft. Popham, etc.	12
Bangor to Bar Harbor	59
" " Castine	59
" " Ellsworth (via Bucksport)	59
" " Field's Pond	57
" " Hermon Pond	57
" " Houlton	67
" " Moosehead Lake (via Dexter)	58
" " Moosehead Lake (via Kenduskeag)	58
" " Phillips Lake	57
" " Pushaw Lake	57
Bar Harbor Side Runs	60
" " to Cherryfield (via Hancock)	59
Belfast Side Runs	54
" to Bangor	57
" " Castine	56

	PAGE
Belfast to Camden (via Lincolnville Centre)	55
" " Cottage City Inn	56
" " Fort Point	54
" " Islesboro	54
" " Liberty	56
" " Lincolnville	55
" " Munroe Village (via Swan Lake)	54
" " Pitcher's Pond	54
" " Tilden's Pond	54
Bethel to Rumford Falls	40
Bethel Hill to Bridgton Centre	40
" " Rangely Lakes	40
" " Rangeley Lakes (via Gorham, N.H.)	41
Bicycle Repairers	67
Biddeford to Alfred	17
" " Biddeford Pool	7
" " Fortune's Rocks	18
" " Goodwin's Mills	17
" " Goose Rocks	18
" " Hill's Beach	17
" " Kennebunkport	18
" " Old Orchard	7, 16
" " Pine Point	16, 18
" " Portland	16
" " Prout's Neck	16
" " Saco Ferry	17
" " Sebago Lake	17
Bingham to The Forks	52
Blaine to Fort Fairfield	68
Boston to Albany	74, 77, 78
" " Chestnut Hill Reservoir	75
" " Dedham	79
" " Fitchburg	74

INDEX.

	PAGE
Boston to Mt. Wachusett	76
" " Nahant	73
" " Portsmouth, N.H.	71–73
" " Providence, R.I.	79, 80
" " Wellesley	75
" " Worcester	75, 76
Bridgton, Attractions of	27
" to Pleasant Mountain	27
" " Summit Spring	27
" " Waterford Flat	27
Brunswick, Points of Interest	31, 34
Brunswick to Augusta	33
" " Bath	42
" " Harpswell	31
" " Mare Point	31
" " Rockland (via Bath)	42
Bryant's Pond to Dixfield	41
" " Rangeley Lakes	41
Bucksport to Castine	59
" " Ellsworth	59
By-Laws, Maine Div. L.A.W.	5
Calais to Houlton	66
" " St. Stephen, N.B.	64
Canadian Tour, Skowhegan Wh. Club	51
Cape Elizabeth and South Portland	20
" " Side Runs	21
Castine to Ellsworth	59
Cathance Lake	63
Charges for Transportation	87
China Pond	44
Cornish	23
" Side Runs	11, 12
" to Bridgton	11
" " Brownfield	11
" " Clark Mountain	12
" " Denmark	11
" " Freedom	11
" " Hiram Falls	11
" " Limerick	11

	PAGE
Cornish to Saco	10
" " Sandy Beach	12
" " Spectacle Ponds	11
" " White Mts	13
Cumberland Mills	22, 25
Delano Park	19
Dennysville to Cathance Lake	64
Dexter to Cambridge	47
Dixfield to Farmington	48
Dover, N.H., to Biddeford (via N. Berwick)	8
Eastport to Calais	65
" " Pembroke	64
Edmundston, N.B., to St. John, N.B.	81
" " River de Loup	69
Ellsworth to Cherryfield (via Hancock)	62
Ellsworth to Machias	62
Emery's Mills to Acton Corner	14
" " Shapleigh Corner	14
Explanation of abbreviations, etc.	6
Fairfield to Skowhegan	44
Farmington to Dixfield	48
" " Strong	48
Field's Pond	57
Fort Fairfield to Andover, N.B.	69
Fryeburg to Bethel Hill	39
Fryeburg to Lancaster, N.H.	26
Gardiner to Augusta	33
" " Togus	33
Gray to Dry Mills	32
Harrington to Jonesport	62
Hermon Pond	57
Houlton to Fort Kent	66
" " Presque Isle	68
" " Woodstock, N.B.	66
Introductory	3
Islesboro	54
Jonesboro to Machias (via Whitneyville)	62
Jonesport "	62
" " Jonesboro	62

89

INDEX.

	PAGE
Kennebunk to Kennebunkport	8
Kennebunkport	7
Land's End (Islesboro)	54
Lewiston Side-Runs	36, 37
" to Augusta (2 routes)	35, 37
" " Brunswick	34
" " Bryant's Pond	35
" " Cobbosseecontee Pond	36
" " Mechanic Falls	38
" " Rangeley Lakes (via Bryant's Pond)	35, 41
" " Sabattus Pond	36
" " Turner	36
Lisbon Falls to Freeport	34
Livermore Falls to Farmington	38
Local Consuls	4
Machias to Calais	64
" " Cathance Lake	63
" " Eastport	63
" " " (via Cutler)	63
" " Jonesport	62
Map I., New Hampshire to Kennebec River	9
Map II., Kennebec River to Penobscot River	42
Map III., Penobscot River to New Brunswick	60
Map, Cape Elizabeth and South Portland	21
" York, Cumberland, Androscoggin and Oxford Counties	31
Milton Mills to Biddeford (via Alfred)	14
Mechanic Falls to Bethel Hill	40
" " " Canton	38
" " " Fryeburg (via Bridgton)	39
" " " North Bridgton	39
Moose River to Moosehead Lake	52
Mount Desert Island	60
New Brunswick Run, A	81, 82
North Berwick to Ogunquit	15
" " " Wells Beach	15
" " " York Beach	15
North Bridgton to Fryeburg	39
Ogunquit Beach	7
Orland to Ellsworth	56

	PAGE
Patten to Houlton	67
Patterson's Bridge to Solon Ferry	52
Pembroke to Eastport	64
Perry to Indian Village	65
Phillips Lake	57
Pittsfield to Carmel	50
Portland Head Light	19
Portland Side-Runs	26, 29
" " to Auburn and Lewiston	32
" " Bath	30
" " Blackstrap Hill (and Monument)	24
" " Bridgton	27
" " Brunswick	31
" " Buena Vista	20
" " Cape Cottage Site	19
" " Cape Elizabeth "Two Lights"	19
" " Coal Kiln Corner	22
" " Cornish	23
" " Duck Pond	24
" " Evergreen Cemetery	22
" " Fryeburg	26
" " Goose Pond	24
" " Harpswell	31
" " Higgins' Beach	21
" " Lancaster, N.H. (via Fryeburg)	26
" " Ocean House Site, Cape Elizabeth	19
" " Old Orchard (reverse No. 7)	16
" " Pine Point (reverse No. 7)	16
" " Presumpscot Falls	29
" " Prout's Neck (via Cape Elizabeth)	21
" " Prout's Neck (via Oak Hill) (reverse No. 7)	16
" " Poland Spring	32
" " Portland Head Light	19
" " Rangeley Lakes	32
" " Scarborough Beach	21
" " Sebago Lake	25
" " Smelt Hill	29
" " Spurwink	21
" " Walnut Hill	29, 30

INDEX.

	PAGE
Portland to Wescustigo Spring	30
" " Westbrook	22, 25
" " White Mountains	13, 26
" " Yarmouth	31
Portsmouth, N.H., to Biddeford	7
Presque Isle to Caribou	69
" " " Caribou (via Washburn)	69
" " " Fort Fairfield	69
" " " Van Buren	69
Pushaw Lake	57
Quantabacook Pond	43
Repairers, bicycle	87
Richmond to Gardiner	33
Rochester, N.H., to Cornish	10
" " " Biddeford (via Sanford)	9
" " " White Mountains (via Cornish)	13
Rockland, Adjacent Points of Interest	53
" to Bangor	53
" " Belfast	53
Road Law	70
Routes in Eastern States	61
Rumford Falls to Bethel	40
Saco to White Mountains	10
St. Stephen, N.B.	64
St. Stephen to St. John, N.B.	65
Sanford to Alfred	9
" " Berwick and Great Falls, N.H.	15
" " Biddeford	9
" " Kennebunk	9
" " North Berwick	15
" " Wells Beach	9
Saturday Cove to Brown's Corner, Northport	53
Schoodic Lakes	62
Searsport Cove to Sears Island	54
Shapleigh Corner	14
Sidewalk Riding, Ethics of	63
Skowhegan to Bangor	50
" " Farmington	48

	PAGE
Skowhegan to Madison Lake	48
" Side-Runs	49
" to Fairgrieves Bay	49
" " Lake George	49
" " Moose River	52
" " Moosehead Lake	51
" " Old Point Monument	49
" " Smithfield	49
South Molunkus to Patten	67
Steep Falls (on Mousam River)	9
Stroudwater	22, 25
Swanville to Monroe	54
The Campaign of Enlightenment. Jas. E. Marrett	86
The Eagle Lake Ride (Bar Harbor)	61
The Green Mountain Ride " "	61
The Ocean Ride " "	60
The 22-mile Ride " "	61
Tilden's Pond	43, 54
Togus to Augusta	33
Turtle's Head (Islesboro)	54
Waldoboro to Belfast	42
Waterville to Bangor	50
" " Belfast	46
" " Fairfield	44
" " Moosehead Lake	47
" " Rockland	45
" " Winterport	46
Wells Beach	7
White Mountain Trips	10, 13, 26
Winterport to Ellsworth	46, 59
Winthrop to Augusta	35
Woodstock, N.B.	68
Woolwich to Rockland	42
Yarmouth to Freeport	31
" " Pownal	30
" " Prince's Point	31
York Beach	7
York County Wheelmen	7

Steinway

Grand Pianos *Upright Pianos*

A splendid assortment of these beautiful instruments is to be found in our warerooms, together with a large and carefully selected stock of the celebrated

HARDMAN **STANDARD**
GABLER **WEBSTER**
BACON *and other first-class*

Catalogues mailed free on application. **Pianos**

Terms:
Cash or Easy Monthly Payments.
Second-Hand Pianos or Organs taken in Exchange.

Would you have the consciousness of having a piano that ranks above every other make? If so, there's only one piano for you. That is the

Steinway

New Upright Pianos to Rent.

Tuning, Repairing and Polishing.

M. STEINERT & SONS CO.

T. C. McGOULDRIC, Mgr.

517 Congress Street,
Portland, Me.

Bicycle Shoes

To enjoy Wheeling to its fullest extent your feet should be covered by the .... L. A. W. BICYCLE SHOE, made of Soft Kangaroo Calf, Low Heel, Lace to the toe.   **Oxfords and Bals.**

Don't Roll Through Portland

Without a visit to our Store, the Oldest and Largest Shoe Concern in Maine. You buy Russets or Patents of us and we will deliver them anywhere in the United States free of charge.

Russets

From $3.50 to $6.00
15 styles.

Palmer Shoe Co.
PORTLAND ME.

Patents

From the Lowest to the Highest,
But never anything but the most sterling leather.

Tennis Shoes

The Best Leather, the Best Rubber, the Best Canvas, are used in our Tennis Goods, and in no class of merchandise does it pay to "Buy the Best" more than in Shoes.

The Sum and Substance

of it is we keep everything in Footwear for Man, Woman, or Child. Send for our Catalogue; we can fit you by mail as well as if you were in our Store.

Wheelmen and Cyclers

Lend Us Your Ears.

WE WILL RETURN THEM WELL FILLED WITH FACTS ABOUT OUR STOCK.

About our
  Witch Hazel and
  Liniments to
  Prevent Lameness.

About our
  Enamel
  Paints
  for Bicycles.

About our
  Cold, Fruity Soda
  as a
  Thirst Quencher.

About our
  Machine Oil
  as a Wheel
  Lubricator.

H. H. HAY & SON,

PORTLAND.   MIDDLE STREET.

Established 1861.   Incorporated 1893.

RANDALL & McALLISTER,

ANTHRACITE AND BITUMINOUS

✻ COAL ✻

CARLOADS A SPECIALTY.

By the Cargo and
at Retail.

**70 EXCHANGE ST. AND
76 COMMERCIAL ST.**

PORTLAND, ME.

ESTABLISHED 1874 — INCORPORATED 1893.

T. B. DAVIS ARMS CO.

193 MIDDLE STREET, PORTLAND, MAINE.

General Agents for Maine, New Hampshire and Vermont for

REMINGTON BICYCLES.

Jobbers of Guns, Rifles, Revolvers, Ammunition, Fishing Tackle, Blasting Materials.

AGENTS LAFLIN & RAND POWDER CO.

HEADQUARTERS FOR . . . . . . **A. G. SPALDING & BROS.'**

**Base Ball, Foot Ball,
Athletic and Gymnasium Goods.**

GLOBE STEAM LAUNDRY

26
28
30
AND
32

T
E
M
P
L
E
S
T

PORTLAND, MAINE.

ONLY HIGH GRADE WORK.

TELEPHONE 316-3.

D. S. WARREN & CO.

Wholesale and Retail Dealers in

ANTHRACITE and

BITUMINOUS

COALS

All Orders by Mail Promptly Filled.

244 Commercial St.,   PORTLAND, ME.

All Wheelmen
Use the . . . .

Preble House,

*The most central Hotel
In the city. . . . . . .*

J. C. WHITE, *Proprietor.*

Monument Square,

*Congress and Preble Streets,
PORTLAND, ME.*

ON arriving in PORTLAND take one of the STEAMERS of the

Casco Bay Steamboat Co.'s Line,

Custom House Wharf,

To see the beauties of CASCO BAY. Two hours' sail.

25c.

First on the Road! First in the Race! First in the Hearts of the Wheelmen!

THE LOVELL DIAMOND

No Better *All Sizes, Styles*

Bicycle Made. *and Prices.*

LIGHT ROADSTER, WEIGHT 21 1-2 LBS.

WE HAVE A LARGE STOCK OF SECOND-HAND WHEELS THAT WE ARE SELLING AT LOW PRICES. SEND FOR LIST.

JOHN P. LOVELL ARMS CO.,
MANUFACTURERS,

Agents Wanted.
Catalogue Free.

———— BOSTON, MASS.

The Thurston Print PORTLAND

TELEPHONE CONNECTION
97 1-2 EXCHANGE ST.

HIGH GRADE
PRINTING
FOR BIKERS

SPECIALTY  Ideas Furnished

FRED. L. TOWER, Pres. & Gen. Man'gr
I. N. HALLIDAY, Supt. & Treas.

D. W. CLARK, President.   M. W. CLARK, Vice-President.

C. B. THURSTON, Treasurer.

The D. W. Clark Ice Co.,

Wholesale and Retail

ICE DEALERS

TELEPHONE, 519-2.

ESTABLISHED 1855.
INCORPORATED 1893.

302 Commercial Street,
PORTLAND, ME.

DENNETT & JOSE,
SURVEYORS, ENGINEERS AND DRAUGHTSMEN,
82 MAIN STREET, SACO, MAINE.

MAINE OUTINGS, MAY NUMBER, HAS THIS TO SAY IN ITS EDITORIAL COLUMN.

THERE are two indispensable articles in the kit of those going into the woods or on the waters which we take pleasure in recommending to sportsmen and campers. We refer to " Camp Comforts" and " Mus-ke-to-ine," prepared by the Stone Chemical Co. of this city. They are inexpensive, occupy little space, and there is no need of suffering the annoyances of insect occupation or stings so long as these preventives are to be found.

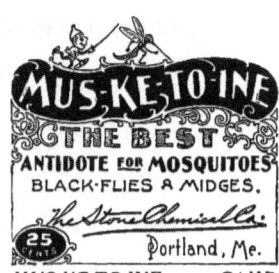

MUS-KE-TO-INE AND CAMP COMFORTS ARE FOR SALE BY ALL DEALERS IN SPORTING GOODS.

PREPARED BY STONE CHEMICAL CO., 90 MIDDLE ST., PORTLAND, ME.

Wheelmen Attention!

When you want to remove that tired, thirsty feeling, always call for

Ingalls Brothers'

Ingleside Spring or Sachs-Pruden's

Ginger Ales.

Sure Cure for Frog in Your Throat.

All the Latest Summer Drinks.

Ingalls Brothers,
  36, 38 and 40 Plum St.,
  Portland, Me.

WINTER CYCLING!

MORRISON'S ADJUSTABLE PNEUMATIC TIRE

ICE CREEPERS.

High speed attainable; absolutely non-slipable; can be adjusted by anyone. . . . .

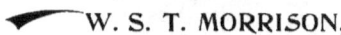 W. S. T. MORRISON,

Originator and Manufacturer.

. . . Also, . . .

Repairer of and Dealer in BICYCLES, Sundries, Sulky-wheels and Pneumatic Tires.

CENTRAL BLOCK,   32 MAIN STREET,

CORNISH, ME.

LAMSON'S LUGGAGE CARRIERS
For all Bicycles.

The Standard and The Best.

For Sale by all Dealers in Cycling Sundries.

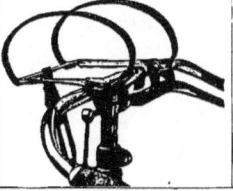

NO. 1. $1.00
This device carries Books, Boxes, and Bundles, and is light, easily applied, and does not rattle.

PRICE No. 4 CARRIER (Drop Front), $1.25
No. 4 DOUBLE, For Two Bundles, 1.50
Send for Descriptive Catalogue.

C. H. LAMSON,
203 Middle St., Portland, Me.

$2.00 AND UPWARDS IN FINE GOLD.

ORIGINATOR OF THE OFFICIAL L.A.W. BADGE.

Send for Circular.

JOHN CALVIN STEVENS,
Architect.

ROOMS 21, 22, 23,
OXFORD BUILDING,

185 Middle Street,

PORTLAND, MAINE.

BUTLER'S BICYCLE HOSPITAL

NO. 64 UNION STREET,

PORTLAND, MAINE.

We have in connection with our Machine Shop a full equipment for the Manufacture and Repairing of Bicycles in all its branches. If a freight train runs over your wheel send us the pieces.

G. W. BUTLER & CO., Portland, Me.

WILLIAM SENTER & CO.

DIAMONDS,

FINE JEWELRY,

WATCHES,

NAUTICAL, OPTICAL AND MATHEMATICAL INSTRUMENTS.

51 Exchange Street, PORTLAND, ME.

SOUVENIR SPOONS IN GREAT VARIETY. A FULL LINE OF TELESCOPES AND MARINE GLASSES.

Sea View Cottage,   =   =

Pond Cove,
Cape Elizabeth, Me.

THIS well-known Summer Resort, under new management, opens for the season June 1; situated on Casco Bay, four miles from city of Portland, two hundred feet frontage on ocean; broad verandas on all floors; superior accommodations, bathing, boating, fishing, billiards and pool; stabling, and all improvements.

The Portland Wheel Club, having made this House their Headquarters. Special Rates will be made to Wheelmen. We make a specialty of Broiled Live Lobsters and Fried Clams.

B. B. Rodick, Proprietor.
E. H. Ingalls, Manager.

YOU should plan your vacation to include

A TRIP DOWN EAST

Put your wheel in a baggage car of the

MAINE CENTRAL RAILROAD

And go to the Rangeley Lakes, Poland Springs, Moosehead Lake, the Crawford Notch, The Dixville Notch, Mt. Desert, and **GOOD** wheel along the **ROADS**

In the White Mountains, along the Maine Coast, among the Lakes Resorts and you can have more good times at small expense than anywhere on the American Continent. Write for tour book and time-tables to

F. E. BOOTHBY, *G.P. & T.A.*,
PORTLAND, ME.

EXCHANGE STREET CAFE,

GEORGE T. MEANS, PROPRIETOR.

FIRST-CLASS SERVICE.

BEST THE MARKET AFFORDS.   43 Exchange Street,

PORTLAND, ME.

We Carry a Very Large Line of

Men's Furnishing Goods

AND WANT YOUR TRADE.

"*Sweaters.*"

Men's Furnishing Department,
EASTMAN BROS. & BANCROFT,
496 Congress Street,
PORTLAND, ME.

MAINE
OUTINGS

READ IT!
——ENJOY IT!

A Monthly Magazine devoted to   *Sports and Outings DOWN EAST.*

Printed on the best book paper and handsomely and profusely illustrated. Our contributors are well-known sportsmen, and writers on outdoor recreation, the lovers of nature of both sexes, who write from experience or observation. Each number contains twenty to forty interesting pages of romance, anecdote, etc., followed by departments devoted to "Rifle and Gun," "Yachting and Aquatics," "Our Field Companions," "Angling," "The Wheel," "Athletics." Each number will contain the latest news from the fish and game regions of Maine, and a faithful report of all events during the concurring month. Have Maine at your fireside each month in the year.

$1.00 PER YEAR. 10 CENTS PER COPY AT NEWS STANDS.

THE MAINE OUTINGS CO.,
———PORTLAND, MAINE.

W E CARRY IN STOCK AN EXTENSIVE LINE OF **BICYCLE TROUSERS**

OF THE VERY BEST MAKE.

IF YOU OR ANY OF YOUR FRIENDS want a pair or a dozen pairs, we should be glad to show you what we've got.

Popular Low Prices, $2.00, 2.50, 3.00, 3.50, 4.00 and 4.50.

ALSO BICYCLE COATS and SUITS. If we haven't the size or sizes in stock we can get them at short notice. Sent C.O.D., privilege of examination, to any address. STRICTLY ONE PRICE.

STANDARD CLOTHING CO.
MAKERS.

255 Middle Street, - - - - - - - PORTLAND, ME.

✻ **If we say** *Our work is better than any other*, you may doubt us.

If we say *Our work is as good as the best*, you *may* believe us. ✻

✻ **If we say** *Compare our work with that which you consider best*, we secure your confidence.

Therefore we say .. We make every variety of Photographs. When you contemplate having pictures, try ours and compare with *others*. We give you a reduced rate check for this purpose. If our work is not *only* as *good*, but *cheaper*, you will patronize us and recommend others.

H. M. Smith

Photographer.

478 Congress St., OPPOSITE PREBLE HOUSE,
PORTLAND, MAINE.

JONES REAL ESTATE CO.,

OFFICE:
208 Middle St., PORTLAND, ME.

Edward C. Jones, President.
Fred E. Jones, Treasurer.

Cottage Lots for Sale and Lease.

200 acres of land on various islands of *Casco Bay*, well situated for *Cottage* and *Hotel* sites.

80 acres on the best part of *Long Island* to be cut into Cottage lots and leased for a term of years. A few Cottages to let on Long Island at moderate prices. *Cottages* will be built to order for parties desiring same on several years' lease.

For full particulars call on or address

EDWARD C. JONES,

208 Middle St., PORTLAND, ME.

If you want the
BEST SHOE

Here It is!

The New

Emerson Gore Bicycle Shoe

Is endorsed by all wearers as the best made "up-to-date." It is stylish, perfect fitting, thoroughly made and constructed on the right principles.

Price: Low Cut, $3.00, High Cut, $3.50.

Sold only through our Emerson Shoe Stores. Send for Spring and Summer Catalogue, and mention *The Wheelman's Road Book.*

R. B. GROVER & CO.,

Makers and Sellers of the Emerson Shoe, BROCKTON, MASS.
Portland Store, under Preble House.

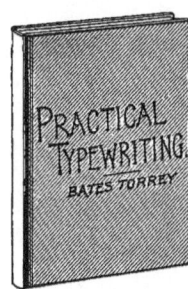

THE
Standard Instructor

in the All-Finger Method of Typewriting.

Third Edition, Revised.

Instruction in Practical Shorthand,

A textbook of Graham Shorthand as taught at Comer's College, Boston.

Price, each $1.50, postpaid.

For particulars regarding textbooks, instruction, business openings and other information about Shorthand and Typewriting, address

BATES TORREY,

566 Washington Street,   **BOSTO**

JOHN MESSING,

Successor to S. A. FLUTSCH.

ORIGINAL - - -

Vienna Café and Restaurant

268 MIDDLE STREET, PORTLAND, MAINE.

St. Julian Hotel.

R. W. UNDERWOOD, PROPRIETOR.

Cor. Middle and Plum Streets,   PORTLAND, ME.

The best arranged hotel in the city, and next block to the Post Office and United States Court Room, and Masonic Hall. Rooms lighted by electricity and heated with steam. A nice billiard hall, hair-dressing room and bath-rooms connected ; in fact every comfort that can be found at any first-class Hotel can be found at the ST. JULIAN. Street Cars pass the door for all stations, steamboat landings, and all points of interest. The only Dining Hall in Portland on the Underwood plan.

WE are prepared to serve Banquets at short notice. Single Lodgings, 50 cts., 75 cts. and $1.00. Rooms, $1.00 per day and upwards.

EVERY BICYCLER

Should use fine *STATIONERY* for correspondence and social purposes. The quality cannot be too fine, nor the style too carefully chosen. The writer, oftentimes, is estimated not only by the language of the note but by the paper on which it is written. People of taste use none but the best, and the best papers to be had are Crane's with "*Hurd's Name on the Box.*" . . . We carry a full line of these superior papers, manufactured by George B. Hurd & Co., in different sizes and tints, and shall be glad to supply you.

STEVENS & JONES COMPANY,
Portland, Maine.

VICTOR BICYCLES ALWAYS LEAD!

HY?

Because the VICTOR is the easiest running Bicycle in the world.

Proved by the Victor Dynamometer, the only machine on earth that actually measures the power required to run a bicycle.

Call and see us before you buy your 1895 mount, so you can buy intelligently. We will take one apart so you can see how well and simply they are made. If gold in Victor bearings would make them wear better we should have it in Victors.

CATALOGUES FREE.

E. S. PENDEXTER,

Congress Street,   PORTLAND, MAINE.

GEORGE E. ELLINGWOOD, President.
CHARLES P. MERRILL, Treasurer.

THE ELLINGWOOD FURNITU[RE CO.]

MANUFACTURERS AND
DEALERS IN GENERAL **HOUSE FURN[ISHINGS]**

Cottage Furniture, Settees, Camp Stools, Morris Chairs, Plush and Leather [...]
Refrigerators, etc

**96 AND 100
EXCHANGE STREET,**   PORTLAND, [ME.]

FACTORY AT HARRISON.

Victors
ALWAYS LEAD!

Why?

Because the Victor is the Easiest-running Bicycle in the World. Proved by the Victor Dynamometer—the only machine on earth that actually measures the power required to run a Bicycle.

www.ingramcontent.com/pod-product-compliance
Lightning Source LLC
Chambersburg PA
CBHW020058170426
43199CB00009B/322